BEVERLEY FRIA___

THE HISTORY AND ARCHAEOLOGY OF AN URBAN MONASTERY

by

Martin Foreman

with graphics by Mike Frankland

Humber Archaeology Partnership
&
Hutton Press Ltd
1998

Published by the Humber Archaeology Partnership,
Kingston upon Hull City Council,
and the Hutton Press Ltd.
130 Canada Drive, Cherry Burton, Beverley
HU17 7SB

Printed and bound by Fretwells Limited, Hull

ISBN 1 872167 95 0

Front cover: The church and main cloister of the
Dominican Friary as they may have appeared in the
first half of the 15th century, looking from the east.
From a photograph of a model of the Friary on
display at the "Old Friary", now the Beverley
Friary Youth Hostel.

Back cover: The Friary, looking from the north,
with the main building of the little cloister in the
foreground. From the model at the "Old Friary".

Contents

	Page
Preface	4
THE WORLD THE FRIARS KNEW	5
A Feudal Society	5
The Monastic Orders	6
England in the 13th Century	7
The Friars	8
The Arrival of the Dominicans in Beverley	9
THE DAILY LIFE OF A DOMINICAN FRIAR	13
A Round of Prayer	13
Friars' Tuck - Food and drink in the Priory	14
Public Works - The Friars in the World	18
THE DEVELOPMENT OF THE BEVERLEY DOMINICAN PRIORY	21
From Humble Beginnings - The Priory in the 13th century	21
Timber Frames - Vernacular Building in Medieval Beverley	25
A Brief Tour of the "Old Friary"	27
Flourishing Friars - The 14th century	33
Stone and Brick in the Priory Buildings	38
The Later Years - The Friars in the 15th Century	44
Dead Patrons Pay - Burial at the Priory	45
The Fading of an Ideal - The Decline of the Priory and the Dissolution of the Monasteries	50
Suggestions for Further Reading	54
Bibliography	55
Acknowledgements	56

Preface

In 1992, at an event marking the publication of a major report by the Humberside Archaeology Unit, it was commented how useful a more accessible version would be to the general reader. The format of archaeological reports makes them valuable to specialist researchers, but tends to deter the rest of us! This is ironic, as archaeology frequently depicts the everyday lives of people who found no place in the records of their own time. And yet, by considering the material evidence for their homes and meals, their work, beliefs and concerns, we draw the very fabric of their world into our own outlook. We recognise common concerns which connect us all, across space and time. Archaeology now fascinates millions, whether as armchair time-travel, or as an unfolding story in which we, too, have a part; or perhaps because it highlights both differences and unexpected similarities between past lifetimes and the modern world.

Following the good advice of our present publisher, we present this book as the "little brother" of a report published in 1996, by Sheffield Academic Press. The reader who finds one of these related books too light or too heavy, for their needs, taste or pocket, may care to turn to the other. Visitors exploring Beverley, and especially its Old Friary, will find this edition a helpful and interesting souvenir. As they follow streets whose course winds down to us from before the friars' time, they will still find their way by the landmarks of a medieval town.

Perhaps most importantly, those fortunate enough to live in Beverley may find this book an illuminating contribution to the understanding of their home. "Beverley - so splendid, so precious" was an epithet first uttered with reference to the exceptional archaeology below their feet. This has accumulated compound interest through the passage of centuries and the remarkable preservation of the most fragile forms of evidence. It will pay dividends to our descendants, however, only if it is cared for. The unseen drying of waterlogged soils can be as devastating as any contentious redevelopment in such an historic location. Informed and responsible stewardship, exercised by the people of Beverley on behalf of us all, will be a most important factor in determining the future of a rich and varied heritage.

Finally, teachers and students in secondary schools, colleges or universities will find a wealth of information between these covers. As well as being a landmark in Beverley today, since 1960 its Dominican Friary has become the most extensively excavated monastery of its type in England. The excavations have been comprehensively reported and analysed, to a modern standard. This study therefore forms an authoritative as well as, we hope, an entertaining introduction to medieval life, and to an important aspect of the making of the English town.

THE WORLD THE FRIARS KNEW

A Feudal Society

The Middle Ages is a term which, in England, describes the centuries between the collapse of Roman rule, after 415 AD, and about 1500 AD. At the beginning of this period, Europe was fragmenting into a shifting patchwork of tribal groups whose identities were frequently uncertain to their contemporaries, let alone to a modern observer. Christianity, which had become the official religion of the later Roman Empire, disappeared with it from most of northern Europe. It would return so successfully that, in 1200, at the height of the Middle Ages, Christendom formed a European community in which every Christian member of society had a place, and whose rulers could frequently converse together in Latin, regardless of their origin. Yet, by 1500, most people in northern Europe would consider themselves as citizens of nation-states, distinguished by their language, culture or institutions from neighbouring countries.

In the Early Medieval period, between about 450 and 800 AD, security was only available under leaders who could command a following of warriors; leaders in turn depended on the loyalty of their men. In return for providing fighters with food and necessities, others could claim their protection, though at the cost of their own independence. These arrangements came to form a highly personalised balance of mutual rights and obligations. A social hierarchy developed, with the war-leader and his household at its summit, and those who toiled to support them at its base. This pattern was endlessly repeated across north-west Europe, increasing in complexity and rigidity with the passage of time, and is known today as the feudal system .

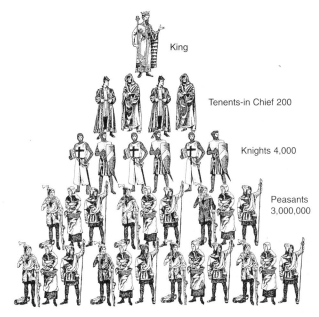

King

Tenents-in Chief 200

Knights 4,000

Peasants 3,000,000

The Domesday Book, a tax-register compiled for William the Conquerer in 1086, gives the first overall view of the feudal system in England. At that time the population of England was about three million. Population rose until the Black Death of 1348-49, when one third of the people of western Europe perished. The resultant labour-shortage was an important factor in the decline of the feudal system.

The Church, having survived the fall of the Roman Empire in the Mediterranean world, embarked on the conversion of the pagans of northern Europe. It directed its efforts at their rulers: once they accepted Christianity, the people could be expected to follow their lead. Conversion would be followed by the establishment of formal administrative structures; bishops were appointed as counterparts to secular rulers, with a parallel jurisdiction over religious matters and property. The earthly power of the Church was advanced through its alliance with kings;

the coronation of the Germanic ruler Charlemagne as "Holy Roman Emperor" by the Pope in the year 800 was an example of this policy, symbolising the marriage of ecclesiastical and secular authority. Charlemagne fulfilled his side of the bargain with ferocious campaigns against subjects or neighbours who proved reluctant to embrace Christianity.

The Monastic Orders

At the forefront of the Church's missionary effort were monks, whose dedication to this perilous task was assisted by their personal commitment to poverty, chastity and obedience - a voluntary rejection of wealth, family ties and self-will which set them apart from others in the interests of faith. Monasticism, a movement named from the Greek monos, meaning alone, had begun in the desert fringes of the Roman Empire, with hermits seeking to live lives of Christian prayer and self-denial. Bands of hermits came together, and rules for communal life, such as that drawn up by St Augustine of Hippo (354-430), in North Africa in the 5th century, provided for material needs without compromising their withdrawal from the world. In his words, these communities formed "Cities of God", as against the towns and cities of the Late Roman world which their members had forsaken.

Orders of monks were established under the authority of the Pope, ensuring that their energies could be directed under such central control as poor communications and frequent disorder permitted. The Benedictines followed the Rule laid down by St Benedict (480-547) in the 6th century. Their communities were governed by an Abbot, from the Hebrew Abba for father, their houses thus being known as abbeys; foundations for women were modelled on equivalent lines, with nuns ruled by an Abbess. Those monasteries founded

in England around the time of the Norman Conquest, such as Westminster Abbey, were mostly Benedictine houses.

An Abbot's deputy was the Prior, or first monk. This term also came to be used for the heads of lesser monastic houses, which would then be known as priories. All such institutions cultivated links with the secular authorities; to secure land for the monks to settle, to protect their fields and flocks, and also the treasures which they accumulated through their own work and through the donations of the pious.

Monks lived in monasteries, in which sleeping and eating areas, rooms for storage and other necessary services, and of course the church, were arranged in a plan which suited their ordered way of life. By about 1100, these would usually be laid out in a fairly standard rectangular arrangement of interconnected buildings, known as a cloister. Other facilities with a less direct connection to the monastic life, perhaps accommodation for guests, or farm buildings, would lie beyond the cloister. The provision of clean water and effective sanitation was a distinctive aspect of monastic planning, and underlined the distinction between those living a regulated life in the cloisters, and the world outside.

A monastery could become a rich institution if well-endowed with property, and if its members were hard-working and scrupulous in observing their personal vows. Material success could weaken the spiritual side of monastic life, and monks sworn to poverty could find themselves leading a more comfortable life than many ordinary folk. Laxity, however, generated reaction from within the Church, which was expressed in periodic movements of reform. One such movement began in the 12th century at Citeaux, in France. The Cistercians took their name from this "mother house", and reasserted monastic seclusion by the remote location of abbeys such as Meaux, between Beverley and Hull, and Fountains, Rievaulx, and Byland in North Yorkshire.

The cycle of monastic zeal, success and decline was a consequence of the engagement of religious institutional life with medieval society. Like all cyclical movements, however, it depended upon the stability of its setting to continue. The medieval world-view was profoundly conservative, and did not admit the possibility of innovation - new ideas would be couched in terms of a return to old ways; or, as intellectual life was dominated by the Church, by reference to Biblical precedent. By 1200, developments which would ultimately sweep away the feudal system were under way. These were reflected by the character of the new religious Orders which sprang up at this time. They would seek involvement with the world rather than fleeing from it, often settling in towns rather than the country; they would enquire into matters of faith; and they would take a positive view of poverty, attempting to write it more effectively into their institutional life. They were the friars.

England in the 13th Century

The friars appeared in the towns of the early 13th century at a time of transition for English society and the Church. Government was becoming more firmly established, royal power in particular being extended through the work of justices, whose judgements contributed to an accumulating body of written law.

The failure of feudal custom to provide reliable troops was promoting a replacement of traditional obligations for cash payment, leading in turn to a widening interest in taxation and economic regulation. An outlet for the energies of a military aristocracy was provided from the 12th century by Crusades. These

initially had high-minded objectives - the protection of pilgrims and the Holy Land. They degenerated into banditry and ill-directed aggression, but at least tended to channel warfare to the fringes of Christendom, and would continue to be promoted to that end long after any prospect of their success had faded.

Churchmen of high rank were drawn from the secular aristocracy; while this ensured respect from their peers, it had also infected religious life with their values. Monastic reform had distanced Orders such as the Cistercians from a corrupting world, but, ironically, their success brought in its train increasing wealth and power. As an institution, the Church was less vulnerable than a noble family to extinction; once acquired by a religious house, property was unlikely to be lost, save by sale or exchange. The literacy of many religious, whether in private, royal or ecclesiastical service, meant that they formed an administrative class, further strengthening the links between Church and secular rulers.

Worldly success undermined the ability of the Church to promote Christian values; as a landholder, it necessarily shared the concerns of secular landlords; with churchmen involved in every level of administration, it could hardly stand aside from political controversy. The Church had most crucially neglected its responsibility for the welfare of the ordinary folk at the base of the feudal system. The parish church was its most usual point of contact with the common people. This had frequently originated as a private foundation; by the 13th century it was often merely one more element of the fund-raising apparatus of local lordship. It would raise a tithe, or 10% tax, on agricultural produce, and levied charges for burial and other services.

The parish church had frequently failed to benefit from the relationship between great lords and the monastic houses which they endowed with lands and gifts; its priests were often ill-paid, uneducated and lax. While monasteries offered lodging for travellers, a dole for the poor, and the colour and ceremony of festivals, these services expended only a fraction of the wealth drawn in from rents, trade and donations.

Most people lived and worked in the countryside, but from before the 11th century, towns had emerged as centres for the processing of rural products, and for trade and exchange. They were often founded by feudal lords, lay and ecclesiastical, to add value to the produce of their lands. Town-dwellers developed an independent outlook, fostered by prosperity and varying degrees of self-government. Their enterprise generated extremes of wealth and poverty cheek-by-jowl; the old safety-net provided by the extended family and customary obligations weakened in this new environment. In wealth or poverty, the urban population was ill-served by a pattern of ecclesiastical provision which had evolved to meet the needs of the lords of a rural population.

The Friars

Unease at the disparity between Christ's emphasis on unworldliness and the life-style of high-ranking churchmen crystallised first in the 12th-century Mediterranean world, where urban development had been most precocious. Francis of Assisi (1181-1226), son of a wealthy urban merchant, "dropped out" to espouse an ideal of dependence upon divine grace: for the Order of friars (from the Latin frater, meaning brother) that he founded in 1209 this was expressed through voluntary reliance on alms. His followers were to adopt a simple habit girdled with a cord, and were popularly known as Greyfriars.

Friars: From left to right, members of the Franciscan, Dominican and Carmelite Orders.

A mendicant, or begging, lifestyle kept the friar humble in his dependence on charity, and attuned to the material and spiritual needs of the poor. Donors could benefit their own souls by their generosity; Christendom benefitted from the zeal of the Franciscans in a field long neglected. Finally, their success posed a timely challenge to the worldly and complacent within the Church itself. Though diluted by practical considerations, emphasis upon poverty and begging remained important to both the Franciscans and the other Orders which their example inspired. The Franciscans first came to England in 1224, and were eventually to have fifty-eight monasteries in England and Wales.

Among the other Mendicant Orders, the most prominent were the Dominicans. Dominic de Guzman (1170-1221), a Spaniard, came to prominence with his attempts to combat the Cathar heresy. This set of views considered the world to be inherently evil, and had gained wide currency in southern France in the early 13th century. Dominic sought to convert the Cathars by argument, though a Crusade was unleashed upon them when this failed, in 1208. The central problem Dominic had identified was that an ill-educated clergy could mount no rational defence of doctrine. The Order he founded in 1216 was dedicated to the salvation of souls by preaching.

Education, through study on the part of friars, and spread to the laity by public speaking, became particularly associated with the Dominicans. Thomas Aquinas (c.1226-1274), a brilliant Dominican scholar, tackled difficulties raised by intellectual examination of faith, and exemplified the Order's approach, which was at once both pious and rational. The Dominicans brought to the mendicant movement an academic flavour which invigorated the universities of medieval Europe. Because of their blend of learning and faith, they were later to acquire a sinister reputation through their deployment as the intellectual shock-troops of the Papacy. They were popularly known as the Friars Preacher, or Blackfriars from the hue of their overgarment. The Dominicans established their first English monastery in 1221, and eventually had fifty-three communities in England and Wales.

Other Mendicant Orders followed in the course of the 13th century. The Carmelite Whitefriars were named after a community on Mount Carmel in the Holy Land. The Augustinian Friars adopted a black habit, and similarly originated from groups of hermits; despite this early interest in seclusion, both Orders were to settle predominantly in towns. The emphasis on begging and preaching was common to all the Mendicant Orders. So, too, was their independence from local ecclesiastical hierarchies: the Provinces,

their administrative bodies at national level, cut across the jurisdiction of bishops and other clergy.

The friars acquired a distinctive role in rejuvenating the sacrament of confession. Like psycho-analysis in more recent times, this flourished especially at a time of urban growth, and afforded support to people drawn from country villages into the more hectic and anonymous life of towns. It was especially helpful to those who had offended against established authorities, though the activity of friars in hearing confessions competed with the work of parish priests and older religious houses.

There were several reasons for the friars to gravitate towards towns. First, there was a new spiritual need to be met. Secondly, a reasonable level of population and prosperity was required if an economic surplus was to be available to support the friars - unlike other Orders, and in keeping with their emphasis on poverty, they did not own land. Most towns had vacant plots within or adjacent to their boundaries, and it was these that were made available to the friars. Thirdly, the position of towns was often dictated by good communications. This enabled the friars to "work" a catchment area, whether harvesting souls or alms. The Dominicans, in particular, were loosely attached to their monasteries; flexible staffing was assisted by their location at strategic points in the medieval network of communications.

The Arrival of the Dominicans in Beverley

The first Dominicans arrived in England in 1221, and had founded a house in Beverley by 1240; a Franciscan monastery was also established there by 1267. Beverley was the foremost town in the East Riding; York and Lincoln were the nearest major urban centres - Hull (then called Wyke) was a waterside settlement at the time, though one that fulfilled an important role in the taxation of trade along the Humber. It would only achieve its official status as the Kings Town on the River Hull at the end of the century. Beverley lay where the dry pastures of the Yorkshire Wolds met the marshy valley of the River Hull. This position offered diverse resources: rural produce including fleeces, fish and fowl; water for the industrial processing of raw materials, and access by river, via the Humber, to much of the North and Midlands.

Beverley traced its origins back over 500 years, to a monastery founded by John, Bishop of York from 705 to 718, who died there. John's reputation for holiness led to canonization, official recognition as a saint, in 1037. St John's tomb had become an assiduously promoted goal for pilgrims, and the magnificent church or Minster in the Early English style - perhaps the fourth or fifth building on the same site - had begun to rise over it at the south end of the town.

By the first decades after the Norman Conquest, the division of Beverley into the long narrow plots of the medieval town had begun. These tenements were occupied by craftsmen and traders: near the Minster, they included workers of cloth and leather. The port of the town, on the Beverley Beck which linked it to the River Hull, was also close at hand. Two marketplaces lay to the north, and the larger, now known as Saturday Market, is thought to have become the commercial hub of Beverley by the 13th century. Between the port and Saturday Market lay a grid of streets, some, like Butcher Row, named after the occupations of those who worked there.

This thriving centre was overseen by the Archbishop of York, the lord of the town, who not only collected rents and dues as he would for any other of his

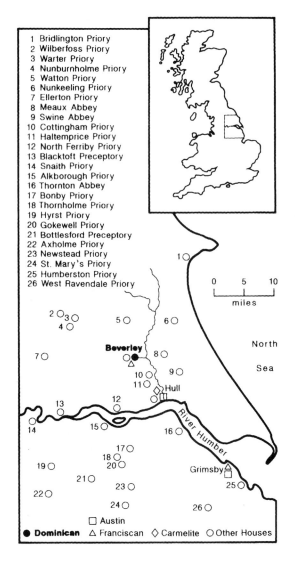

1 Bridlington Priory
2 Wilberfoss Priory
3 Warter Priory
4 Nunburnholme Priory
5 Watton Priory
6 Nunkeeling Priory
7 Ellerton Priory
8 Meaux Abbey
9 Swine Abbey
10 Cottingham Priory
11 Haltemprice Priory
12 North Ferriby Priory
13 Blacktoft Preceptory
14 Snaith Priory
15 Alkborough Priory
16 Thornton Abbey
17 Bonby Priory
18 Thornholme Priory
19 Hyrst Priory
20 Gokewell Priory
21 Bottlesford Preceptory
22 Axholme Priory
23 Newstead Priory
24 St. Mary's Priory
25 Humberston Priory
26 West Ravendale Priory

Friars settled only in the major ports of the region - first Beverley - linked to the Humber by the Beverley Beck and the River Hull - then Grimsby and Hull. The majority of longer-established monasteries lay in the countryside; many owned large and productive estates.

manors, but also levied tolls on goods brought to market. The regulation of important crafts had long been delegated to the merchants: Beverley's 12th-century "Statute of Weavers" is the earliest surviving English example of a code of restrictive practices, and by 1163 the quality of Beverley cloth had been recognised by Royal Charter.

The Archbishop, as landlord, granted the Dominican friars a damp and empty site behind industrial tenements fronting onto Eastgate, north-east of the Minster. The original extent of their land is uncertain, though it was eventually to amount to a total of four and a half acres. It was separated from the tenements by a polluted drain, perhaps the Walkerbeck, but this would merely have enhanced an atmosphere already thick with the stench of cloth and leather steeping in urine and excrement, of boiling dye-vats, and of the rubbish generated by such activities.

Premises involved in cloth and leather processing made poor neighbours, even to medieval sensibilities, and were often located down-wind from the rest of a settlement. Should the wind have shifted to the east, the smoke from pottery and tile kilns along the Beverley Beck would have drifted across the friars' site. The Archbishop may have taken a measure of satisfaction from the insalubrious setting which he was able to provide for the latest exponents of holy poverty: at much the same time as the friars were settled on the east side of Beverley, he was moving his own local residence from the bustling Saturday Market to Hall Garth, by the leafy glades of his new deer-park.

Apart from these aspects of the site, which would have pleased the most austere of early friars, it also had its good points. Religious houses lay to the north - the Preceptory, or regional headquarters, of the Knights Hospitaller; to the east - the church and hospital of St Nicholas (the term "hospital" embraced everything from hostels to quasi-monastic institutions for the care of the poor or sick); and to the south-west - the Minster and its associated properties. The Dominicans therefore found themselves part of a developing religious enclave.

The present Minster was under construction throughout the 13th century, so a body of masons would have been intermittently available; the Dominicans were almost certainly beneficiaries of their skill. The Beverley Dominicans cultivated links with the nearby maritime community, being called on to preach at ports in the region in the 13th century. Their church was accessible to the public from what is still called Friars Lane, and, perhaps later, from Eastgate. The traffic of pilgrims to the shrine of St John would have been available to swell both their income and their congregation.

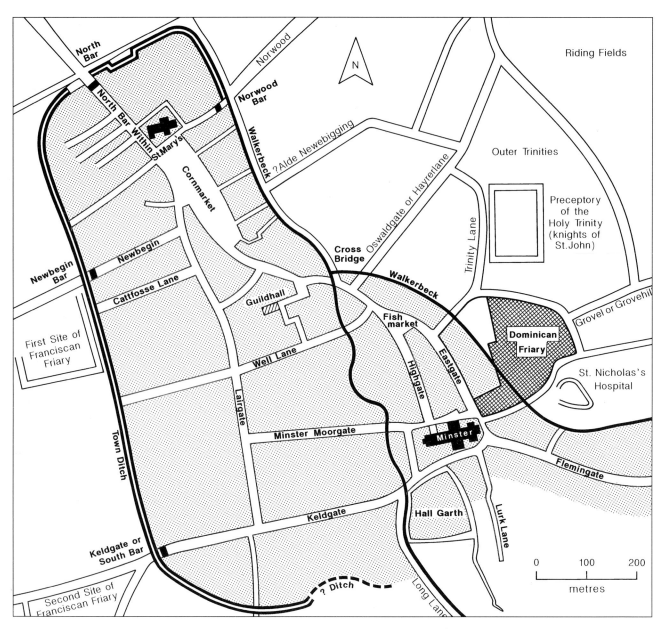

A simplified plan of medieval Beverley, based on Miller et. al. 1982.

THE DAILY LIFE OF A DOMINICAN FRIAR

Like other Orders of monks and nuns, the Dominicans lived by a Rule. This set out the order of tasks and duties through the day, in a timetable which would - in theory - only be relaxed for the sick and the old, or by special dispensation. The Rule adopted by Dominic was that which had been composed by St Augustine. This was also followed by other Orders, as the practical requirements for the regulation of a religious house would often be similar: the aim was to enable a communal life of poverty, chastity and obedience.

More distinctive aspects of Dominican practice were laid down by their Constitutions: these decreed limitations on the size, decoration and magnificence of their buildings, and detailed their administrative arrangements. The Constitutions established a system of checks and balances with a democratic flavour, intended to prevent individuals in the Order's hierarchy from exerting undue personal influence.

The principal officer of each monastery was the Prior - hence the formal designation of a friars' house as a Priory. The Prior appointed subordinate officials from among the brethren, in some cases through rotation of offices. The Constitutions were intended to permit the implementation of the Rule, and to prevent the Order compromising its ideals through worldly success.

A Round of Prayer

The Dominican's day was structured around episodes of communal prayer, rather than the sunrise-to-sunset regime of the working man. The times for prayer, or "hours" (most were fairly short) were signalled with a bell, their timing adjusted to the latitude and the season. Their Latin names, which related to a notional twelve hours of daylight, were the same as those used in other monasteries. Other duties or study had to be fitted in between these fixed points, of which Mass and Compline were the most important to Dominicans. The approximate sequence of a typical day, in summer, and expressed in modern terms, was as follows:

4 AM: On the sound of the bell for morning Matins the friars rose immediately, having five or ten minutes to dress and make their way to the church while privately reciting the prayers of their Office; they then took their places in stalls in the choir (that part of the church set aside for the use of the friars, at its east end). They recited prayers silently, and then chanted psalms led by a single voice, with alternating choruses from either side of the choir; the friars rose to sing and sat down again as the verses were picked up by those opposite. The same order of prayer and chant was followed for all the "hours" of prayer.

5 AM: Sung Mass; the celebration of a communion service. A later or additional Mass might be held at a time when the laity could more easily attend.

6 AM: *Prime* (the first hour of the day): communal prayer in the choir.

7 AM: Friars went from church to Chapter, the regular meeting for the administration of daily business. It was named from the widespread custom of reading a chapter of the monastic Rule every day, though the Dominicans did not stress this tradition. The meeting was held in the Chapter House, which always lay on the east side of the cloister as a building which projected back from the east side of the cloister, conveniently close to the choir. A sermon would be preached here on important days, and a daily recital included the saints and martyrs of the day - who were regarded as available in Heaven to help with earthly matters - and prayers for benefactors. This was followed by correction by the

Prior, when practical matters would be dealt with. Novices, those trainee-friars who had not yet taken their final lifelong vows, then withdrew. Then, professed friars made open confession of their faults. (Meetings in chapter became weekly rather than daily after the 13th century, when recitals would take place in the church.)

8 AM: Free time; spent in study, rest, or private devotion. Such intervals might also offer an opportunity for a light cold snack, if this was required to prevent fainting or a loss of concentration - monastic Rules aimed to avoid unhealthy excesses of behaviour which would detract from the physical or mental health of members of the community.

9 AM: *Terce* (the third hour): communal prayer in the choir.

12 PM: *Sext* (the sixth hour): communal prayer in the choir.

3 PM: *None* (the ninth hour): communal prayer in the choir.

3.30 PM: Dinner was a communal meal in the refectory, or dining room. Silence would be observed, though instructive texts would be read to the friars while they ate. A rest period would be allowed after dinner.

6 PM: Vespers: communal prayer in the choir.

7 PM: Compline: though usually a minor "hour" of communal prayer, this was the most important one to the Dominicans because lay people could attend after work. As chanted prayer reached its climax, the screens between the choir and the nave of the church (the area for the public) were opened, and the friars went in procession to the nave; all assembled knelt, and were solemnly blessed. After singing, the friars returned to the choir to complete their prayers. A period for individual devotions followed.

8 PM: On a signal - often the rattling of keys - all retired to the dormitory to sleep; the scrupulous might discreetly undertake penance: self-discipline with a whip or rod, or perhaps the adoption of some uncomfortable posture for prayer, so as to make amends for personal weakness or failings.

12 PM: Midnight Matins: the friars rose from sleep, to go to the choir for communal prayer, afterwards returning to rest for about three hours before beginning the round of "hours" again.

If adhered to faithfully, this was a demanding schedule. Prayer, however, was the central duty of any monk or nun. The application brought to prayer enhanced the effectiveness of all other works - a view of the interconnected nature of all things which lay at the heart of medieval belief. To neglect prayer was frequently considered the worst failing of which those in religious Orders could be guilty. Not only did it undermine their activity in the world, but it also breached the contract whereby they were supported by society, in order to pray and work for its spiritual and earthly welfare.

Friars' Tuck - Food and Drink in the Priory

The food waste recovered from excavations casts a fascinating light on the nature of a friar's dinner. According to their Constitutions, the friars were meant to observe perpetual abstinence. Abstinence was defined as the avoidance of "flesh-meat" from four-legged animals; as birds have only two legs, eating chicken, duck or goose would not violate this rule. Fish, especially eel and herring, was prominent in the friars' diet.

This restricted diet was not unique: all Christians were meant to abstain from meat on Wednesdays, Fridays and Saturdays, and the pious would extend this penance throughout Lent, a season of nearly two months before Easter. As animals reared for food were usually slaughtered in November, to avoid the expense of winter fodder, fresh meat would be available only to the rich in the early months of the year.

Fish was widely consumed, fresh from the sea in a

port like Beverley, or where, as at the Priory, fishponds were available. Fishes were also carried live in barrels packed with wet straw, or dried and salted, to inland places. Shellfish, especially oysters, were universally consumed, only having become a delicacy in recent times. Chicken and eggs were, however, more prominent on the friars' table than elsewhere, and their abundance may provide the best evidence that they adhered to a regulated diet.

Despite the Dominicans' Constitutions, not all meals served at their Beverley Priory were meat-free. Meat bones were abundant in a late-13th-century building serving either as a refectory (dining room) or an infirmary (for the care of the old or the sick). In the latter case, this might reflect the more relaxed regime permitted for the infirm. In the later 14th and 15th centuries mutton became prominent in the diet of friars, here and elsewhere in the north of England. Its availability or cheapness may have encouraged relaxation of the rules, perhaps arising from its frequent donation by benefactors.

Meat usually came jointed, from the local market, so the scandal of slaughtering animals for food on the premises of a formally abstinent monastery was avoided. Hunted game such as deer, which was commonly eaten in wealthier institutions in Beverley, was not found here. In the later medieval period, the spirit of restricted diet was better observed than the letter of the law of abstinence.

The recovery of waterlogged remains preserved in cess-pits in Beverley balances what would otherwise be a very distorted archaeological picture of medieval diet. Bread was a staple food, eaten year-round, and contributed masses of cereal bran to samples of cess-pit fills examined in the laboratory. For the later winter months a near-vegetarian diet would have been normal. This would have been especially important at the Priory, given the restrictions that the friars placed on their own diet. Gifts of corn to the friars between 1314 and 1320 suggest that they had a bake-house; in 1493 corn and malt were provided, showing that brewing also took place on the premises.

Peas and beans, which could be dried if not eaten fresh, were also important. Seasonal fruits and nuts would supplement this diet; these included figs and peaches as well as berries from woods and hedgerows. The friars also had orchards and gardens within their precinct, so fruit and vegetables could be home-grown.

Although the friars were exceptional in having installed a piped water supply to their house, drinking untreated water would have been a risky business in

Pounding apples in a stone trough, to extract juice for cooking or cider-making. Hard work - perhaps done by a lay brother...

a medieval town, with its inadequate sanitary provision. Ale, or beer (the same malt-based drink flavoured with hops or other plants such as nettles), was universally consumed: the boiling of the ingredients rendered them safe, while the alcohol present had antiseptic properties. Cider was also a popular beverage; like ale or beer, the cider for everyday use would be weak, if safe.

... While quality control was a more responsible task - a friar would fill the cellarer's office!

Wine imported from France was widely consumed, this trade being marked by distinctive jugs brought along with the wine to this country. Examples were found in the Priory, along with fragments from an expensive Venetian glass goblet. The latter may, however, have been brought (and broken) by a visitor rather than by the friars.

Cooking in a house of friars took place in a kitchen building. At Beverley this probably lay on the west side of the cloister, and took the form of a long building with a large fireplace, and channels for liquid waste leading out through its wall to a drain beyond. A circular stone tank outside may have held

water for kitchen use, or could have served for keeping live fish in water, to assure their freshness (wooden tanks could also be used for this, and examples of these have been excavated in Hull). Cooking and serving food would have been the responsibility of lay-brothers or servants rather than the friars themselves.

Up to the 14th century, food could be spit-roasted if meat or poultry, baked in flat dishes if fish, or, most commonly, as vegetables made up the larger part of diet, boiled in a stew. Ovens used for baking bread were also used for the preparation of other dishes; pies were popular, eaten either at table or sold by street-vendors as "take-away" food.

Left: Pounding meat, mutton at the later Friary, and grinding food in a mortar; Centre: Cooking stews in large pots. Right: basting chickens as they roast on a spit.

In the course of the 14th century, frying became more common, and from this time fragments of earthenware frying-pans appear among finds. This fashion of cooking was introduced into England from the Low Countries, perhaps as a result of the increasing range of imported spices which were becoming available, traded overland from the Far East and reaching northern Europe via the Mediterranean: the intense heat of frying helps to flavour food with spices. Coriander, dill, garlic and poppy have all been recovered from waterlogged cess-pit deposits in Beverley, showing that a taste for spicy food was well-established in the town. Strict penalties existed for the sale of bad meat, so the medieval use of spices was probably the result of a preference for tasty dishes, rather than for the salvaging of rotten food.

Cooked food was carried from the kitchen to the main refectory, to the infirmary refectory if it did not have its own kitchen; and to visitors or friars eating privately in their rooms. Private meals represented a relaxation of the monastic Rule, as they would involve eating outside the refectory, in a less formal setting; this became more common from the later 14th century.

At this time, the preparation of cooked food for table seems to have taken place at one end of the refectory building, as bones from fish-heads and fish-tails found there outnumbered those from edible parts. Servers would then bring food to table through doors at one end of the dining area. In the 13th century, it is possible that the Prior ate apart from the other friars at a high table, on a slightly raised platform at one end of the room.

The 14th-century refectory had benches round its walls, at tables, so friars would sit around the outside of the room, facing into its centre, leaving room for food to be brought to them. Pottery is one of the most common finds from archaeological excavations, but this merely reflects its durability, and most tableware was of wood. Dishes and bowls were lathe-turned in ash, but also in maple, willow or oak.

The tables sometimes faced a central fireplace. Chicken-bones or small scraps were sometimes thrown into the fire rather than being cleared away; some which fell short have been recovered! The large flat fireplaces common in 13th and 14th-century Beverley were well-adapted to burning peat, which was extensively dug locally. Coal was brought down

Preparing fish: at the Beverley Friary, cooked fish was "topped and tailed" in a chamber at one end of the dining room.

from County Durham from the 14th century, and brushwood might also be collected as fuel. Smoky fires could make meal-times uncomfortable, and in the 14th-century infirmary refectory at Beverley this led first to the construction of draught-excluding screens, and when these proved inadequate, to the blocking of a doorway.

The floors of some eating areas were strewn with reeds; these would probably be lain across each other so that, when trampled, they formed a naturally woven mat. This could then be rolled up and replaced periodically, in effect more like a carpet than a stable floor. Other buildings, including the kitchen, would be flagged with plain red tiles, while the main refectory from the later 14th century may have had floorboards in the centre of the room, and tiles beneath the tables and benches. The tiles here might have been plain, or might alternatively have formed a simple chequer-pattern of yellow and green.

The little cloister dining room, with brick bench-footings round three sides of the room. The draught-excluder ran from the hearth (centre) to a doorway (top right), which was later blocked up.

The rule of silence at table, and the reading of passages from the Bible or other devotional works, was common in monastic life. The friars made architectural provision for this. The later-14th-century refectory at Beverley had a projecting foundation at one side, for a pulpit built into the thickness of its wall. A window behind the reader would light his text: as the formal meal-time was in the early afternoon, natural light from a large window at its east end would suffice for illumination of the refectory.

The evidence from cess-pits has been recurrently cited above; this is a particularly important aspect of the archaeology of various sites in low-lying Beverley, as organic remains which would normally rot away may be preserved where air is excluded by the waterlogging of soils. These remains not only include pips, stones and roughage passed through medieval bowels, but also the eggs of the internal parasites with which medieval people were regularly infested. These included whipworms and tapeworms, whose eggs are only detectable through microscopic examination.

The processing of food often left other contaminants to be eaten. Corn-cockle occurs naturally with bread-wheat and has repeatedly been found in Beverley, while ergot fungus (a natural source of LSD) grows on rye which has become damp. Though innocuous in small amounts, either plant could induce convulsions or hallucinations if present in quantity. St Anthony's Fire was a mysterious medieval condition which afflicted whole communities with hysteria or visions, and such outbreaks may have been caused by seriously contaminated grain.

Public Works - The Friars in the World

Duties outside the house were much more important to the friars than to other Orders, as their life was directed to "outreach" work in their host communities. These duties centred on the combination of preaching and hearing confessions. In 1301, ten Beverley Dominicans, of a total of thirty-six resident in the house at the time, were licensed to take confessions and grant absolution, or forgiveness of sins.

Private study in the monastery occupied much of the friars' time between the "hours" of prayer. This enabled the composition of sermons drawing on both Scripture and exempla, or instructive tales. A successful sermon for a Dominican preacher was one that inspired members of its audience to recognise and admit their sins, which could then be privately confessed to him. Confession would be followed by the grant of absolution, which wiped the spiritual slate clean. Penance would be allocated, as payment for absolution. This might be prayer, or some good work offered in compensation for past wrong-doing, and perhaps to correct its worldly consequences. It left the repentant sinner free of guilt, in the eyes of God and his or her own conscience.

A friar could hear confessions in peoples' homes...

The Dominican Constitutions carefully stipulated that this religious work should be distanced from the gathering of alms, and dictated that a friar working outside the monastery should always be accompanied by another. The failure to observe these precautions often led to impropriety - especially when the more attractive sinner was closeted with a lone friar, or when the rich were encouraged to signal their repentance by alms-giving. An English Dominican complained that "Preachers boast more readily of the donations they have received than of the confessions they have heard". The privacy and frankness of the confessional situation lent itself to some abuse, and much more widely-held suspicion.

Later friars found mounting competition from peddlers of indulgences, a "get-out-of-gaol card" to buy off a penance, or even to reduce time spent in purgatory after death. Such exploitation of weakness and credulity was sponsored by ecclesiastical authorities hungry for cash, from the Papacy downwards, in the later medieval period.

Aside from these duties, and unlike members of many other Orders, the Dominicans did not usually work, except as chaplains or tutors; positions where their religious or educational functions were pre-eminent. Such practical tasks as were necessary to the functioning of the monastery fell to friars serving as office-holders in rotation, who would not engage in preaching, or to lay-brothers.

The lay-brothers had not taken full monastic vows, but lived within the house as servants, making up about 10% of the Order's numbers. Cooking or mending of garments was probably the responsibility of lay-brothers at Beverley, and it appears that women were never employed within the monastery. Lay-brothers were also intended to take a leading part in the gathering of alms. Successful begging was, however, a skill in itself, and one which was necessary for the survival of the community. This demarcation of duties was always ill-defined - St Dominic himself had gone "from door to door seeking alms, and he received bread as a poor man". Collections would be made by friars with a sack for offerings; either calling on households, or stationed in some busy spot on a market or festival day.

.... Sometimes with unfortunate results.

Geoffrey Chaucer, in his Canterbury Tales, written in the 1380s, gives a vivid picture of a pair of friars and their servant at work on their collecting round. He puts his description into the mouth of a Summoner, an official working for a bishop's court - which dealt particularly with sexual misdemeanours - and hence himself representing another class of unpopular religious hangers-on:

"With scrip and pointed staff uplifted high
He went from house to house to poke and pry
And beg a little meal and cheese, or corn.
His comrade had a staff was tipped with horn,
And bore a pair of ivory tablets, jointed,
Also a stylus elegantly pointed.
He always wrote the names down as he stood
Of those who gave him offerings or food
(in Pretence of praying for them by and by)
'Give us a bushel of barley, malt or rye,
A wee God's cookie, then, a slice of cheese,
It's not for us to chose, but as you please;
A penny to say mass, or half a penny,
Some of your brawn perhaps - you haven't any? -
Well then, a bit of blanket, worthy dame
Our well-beloved sister! There's your name,
It's down. Beef? Bacon? Anything you can find'.
A sturdy varlet followed them behind,
The servant for their guests, and bore a sack,
And what they gave he carried on his back."

THE DEVELOPMENT OF THE DOMINICAN PRIORY

The buildings of the friars were arranged so as to help them to live an ordered domestic life, and played a vital part in the functioning of their monastery. The modification of the buildings closely related to changes in the size, activity and character of the community. The remains above-ground include only elements of the precinct wall and the "Old Friary" - which may in fact have been built after the friars' time. Excavations at Beverley between 1961 and 1989, however, have given a uniquely detailed view of the structural development of the house, and hence afford an insight into its history. This spanned the 13th to 16th centuries: from the first years of the Dominican mission, through the relaxation of standards of austerity in the later Middle Ages, to the final expulsion of the friars and the ruin of their priories at Henry VIII's Dissolution of the monasteries (1535-39).

From Humble Beginnings - The Priory in the 13th Century

When the friars arrived in Beverley they would initially have required a roof over their heads and, to achieve their spiritual objectives, a church for communal and public worship. As building work at a mendicant house depended on donated funds, cheap wooden buildings were put up, and served until their replacement in stone could be afforded. Traces of a timber building supported by sill beams and posts close to the stone church might represent its temporary predecessor. A similar form was also adopted for an open hall which stood about fifty metres to the north, on an alignment matching that of the church. The most likely use for this building was

as a communal refectory. It stood beyond the site designated for the construction of other ranges, so that it could be used until these were ready.

The preferred form for any monastery was the cloister: a rectangular arrangement of ritual and functional buildings. The friars adapted this arrangement to the particular circumstances of their site. At Beverley, the position of a drain along the west edge of their precinct dictated that toilets and kitchens should lie on the west side of the cloister. This, in turn, limited options for the placement of the dormitory, requiring access to the toilets, and the refectory, served by the kitchen - one or other of these lay on the north side of the cloister. The ritual functions of the choir and chapter house, on the other hand, were less flexible; as usual, these lay to the east.

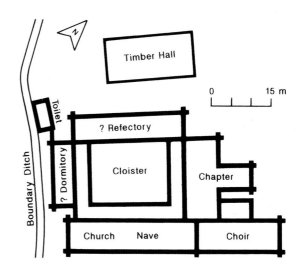

The layout of the Beverley Dominican Friary, in the form it had achieved by about 1275.

The west end or preaching nave of the Friary church. The original part built in the 1240s continues under the "Old Friary's" new shower block (top); the extension of the early 1300s was in matching style.

The choir formed the east end of the church, which lay on the south side of the cloister, completing the enclosure of a garth or lawn.

The first structure to be raised in stone would have been the church. This was a simple long rectangular building divided into two parts: the friars' choir to the east and, separated from it by screens, the nave for public worship. An open, well-lit, nave permitted preaching to be seen and heard by a large congregation. This was a particular feature of friars' churches, and was imitated by the builders of later medieval urban churches, such as Hull's Holy Trinity. Despite the simplicity of its plan, close-jointed masonry shows that the church was expertly constructed.

Painted decoration frequently covered the internal walls of churches, in colours which would appear garish to a modern eye. The friars' church may have been painted with lurid narrative scenes - the Last Judgement became a favourite theme in the 14th century - to teach and impress those who attended services there. The bare walls of medieval churches today reflect recent fashion rather than their original decor. Painted plaster which survives in the "Old Friary", dating to either shortly before or after the departure of the friars, gives an impression of motifs which were both decorative and allegorical.

In the 15th century a statue of St Mary stood in the middle of the nave, and a basin for holy water by the south door. These are the only fixtures whose position within the church, in its later form, is known. It is likely that a range of tomb monuments may also have accumulated by this time, cluttering what had originally been an open area. Save, perhaps, for ledges round the walls, seating would not have been provided.

The fine stonework of the toilet, stained by nearly three centuries of use. Chutes emptied onto chalk paving which was flushed clean by a channelled stream, now passing under the "Old Friary".

The high quality of stonework on the church was surprisingly matched by that seen in the toilet block (or reredorter), suggesting that this facility was also early work. The church, central to the life and image of the community, would be built as well as possible. The fine construction of the toilet, however, can hardly be explained in these terms. Its significance lies in its association with the dormitory which it was intended to serve, and whose early structure was itself to be concealed by later building work. It indicates that skilled masons, perhaps drawn from those employed on the rebuilding of the Minster,

designed and began the construction of the first stone cloister.

A unity of design is suggested by the consistently high quality of stonework on the south side of the cloister (the church) and to the west (the toilet, and by implication the range that it served). The early north range of the cloister had a similar internal width to that of the church, and so may have been planned at the same time.

The completion of the cloister, however, was a drawn-out affair; a royal gift of fifteen oaks in 1263 may have been to complete the roofing of one of the later parts to be built. Window glass found elsewhere, but probably originating in the cloister, was decorated with line-painted designs favoured in the mid-to-late 13th century. This indirect evidence suggests that the cloister was glazed, and hence near-complete, by that time. The timber hall thought to have served as a "temporary" refectory was pulled down around 1275, so this may hint that it had at last been replaced by a stone building forming part of the cloister.

It is possible that the cloister buildings had vaulted ceilings. Alleys may have run through them at ground floor level, linking the various ranges. The friars' church formed the south side of the cloister, with an east end that extended beyond the quadrangle of other buildings. Opposite the church lay another major building, probably the refectory. To the east, the chapter house projected back from another range, whose use is uncertain. To the west, ground-floor kitchens may have had a dormitory over them at first-floor level. Externally, paired buttresses supported the corners of each building; a convention also followed by later work.

Clear window glass, with red-painted motifs designed to be silhouetted against daylight. These were mostly floral and vine-tendril patterns. The gridded background is dated to the 1250s; plainer pieces show more naturalistic forms of the later 1200s and 1300s. Lower rows include border pieces, and plain glass of the 1300s still set in its lead cames.

The later alteration of the buildings has left the original positions of the dormitory and refectory uncertain. It is, however, known that the position of the toilet must have dictated amendment of the more usual monastic plan, in which the dormitory would lie on the east side of the cloister. This flexibility was typical of the friars' houses; a Dominican of the mid 13th century reported that "We have nearly as many different plans and arrangements of our buildings and churches as we have priories". The toilets and kitchen drains emptied into a muddy stream-course, the toilet being "flushed" by the stream. A piped water supply probably fed a cistern in the middle of the cloister, with conduits leading from it to other parts of the house.

The detached timber hall was rebuilt shortly after 1275 on an alignment which was skewed away from that of the cloister, a feature which may have underlined its separation from the regulated community. The new hall was an aisled building, a style carrying some implications of status and appropriate to communal life, but one which was passing out of use in secular society by the later 13th century. This form was, however, associated with monastic infirmaries. Some proportion of the community must by this time have been too old and frail to cope with the full rigour of monastic life. A separate refectory may have been provided for them; as noted above, meat-bones were found in the silts which accumulated on the floor.

In 1299 the Priory housed thirty-three residents. By this time, its buildings comprised a modest stone church and cloister, and a new timber hall beyond it. Provincial Chapters of the English Dominicans had been held at Beverley in 1240 and 1286. The Priory would have been unrecognisable to a friar returning to Beverley in 1286, had he attended the first meeting as a novice.

Timber frames - vernacular building in medieval Beverley

Our view of medieval architecture today is inevitably coloured by the most conspicuous buildings of the period which now remain: principally churches and castles built in stone. These, however, give a very misleading picture as to the style and appearance of medieval houses and work-places, built for vernacular, or every-day, use.

The majority of respectable buildings erected in Beverley before 1400 were framed in timber, which provided a prefabricated skeleton to be clad with

Men at work building a very respectable three-storey house - the straight timber would be especially costly. Note how the master carpenter isn't getting his hands dirty...

lighter materials. The structural techniques employed in timber framing were not dissimilar to the modern use of steel girders. Such timber frames might be walled with interwoven sticks forming wattle - often plastered with clay to make wattle-and-daub; with turf; with planks, or even mud blocks. A more humble dwelling might barely last for the lifetime of its builder if not carefully maintained, and its roof and walls would have been framed with poles rather than beams. The fragility of these materials means that evidence for their use survives only on archaeological sites, rather than in standing buildings, though ancient building methods have survived into relatively recent times in rural areas.

A further misconception is that medieval England was densely wooded. The English countryside has seen clearance and intensive use over the last six thousand years. When William the Conqueror sought to indulge his passion for hunting, this could only be accomplished by the eviction of villagers and the creation of a wilderness: the New Forest. Similarly, the Archbishop of York's deer-park at Beverley was created from old pastures in the 13th century, rather than by the enclosure of primeval woodland. Medieval agriculture involved the cultivation of large open fields, and in the later 13th and 14th centuries took in marginal land at the expense of such forest as remained.

By this time, large native-grown timber was becoming scarce. Hence Baltic oak, from what is now northern Germany, Estonia, Latvia and Lithuania, was imported on a large scale into ports such as Hull in the 14th and 15th centuries. Sophisticated techniques to join timbers were developed in response to the scarcity and value of the raw material rather than because of its abundance. Even in the 13th century, it was only a gift of fifteen oaks in 1263 - felled in the royal forest of Galtres, outside York - that allowed the friars to complete the roofing of their new monastery at Beverley.

Methods to prolong the life of structural timbers were developed, though older styles might continue in use if a building was cheap, of low status, or built of reclaimed materials. Again, surviving examples of medieval carpentry are usually to be found only in churches or the later-medieval houses of the wealthy, or on waterlogged archaeological sites. Only the latter are truly representative of everyday building techniques. Medieval carpenters were skilful and respected technicians who commanded higher wages than labourers, but their work survives rarely because of the hazards of fire and the vagaries of fashion and rebuilding.

Archaeological evidence for timber buildings usually consists of elements of their ground-plans, from which the nature of the superstructure must be inferred. In Beverley, from the 9th century to the 12th, the ground-plan of smaller buildings was sometimes defined by sill beams, straight timbers laid on or in the ground, from which vertical members would rise. In such a structure, verticals carried the weight of the roof down to the sill beam.

For a larger building, posts might be set directly in the ground; in such cases their positions, or post-pits, show the limits of the main frame. The insubstantial walls of such buildings would serve only as screens, without a load-bearing function. Their position is sometimes suggested only by the limits of deposits which accumulated within a building. Curved beams might be used in cruck construction, which was a down-market technique using cheaper timber; this persisted into later centuries in the countryside. Whether straight or curved beams were available, the spaces between paired timbers formed bays, or cells. These might define rooms when the building was

occupied, though open-plan living was usual in a hall. It was the sill-beam technique, with a stony footing serving as a damp-course to prolong the life of the wooden beam, which was used to build the friars' first refectory at Beverley. The building stood for about forty years.

From the 11th century, in buildings erected for richer patrons, vertical posts set in parallel rows would support straight horizontal timbers, on which roof timbers would rest. The bases of the posts would be set in pits packed with rubble for stability. Damp would inevitably promote decay where the post entered the ground: a post of oak one foot square

continued on page 30

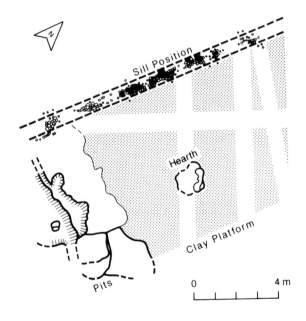

The 13th-century timber hall built on sills - a temporary dining room? Pits may mark soakaways for a hand-basin. Washing before meals was a ritual cleansing; its benefits to health were not clearly understood in the medieval period.

A BRIEF TOUR OF THE OLD FRIARY

The "Old Friary" is a splendid but mysterious building. It is uncertain whether it dates to the time of the friars, or whether it was built using materials robbed from their house after 1539. The standing walls rest on medieval foundations, at least at its eastern end. Their position, apart from the cloister, may indicate that the original building served as a guest-house - as its successor still does today.

The brick-built side of the "Old Friary" as the visitor first sees it today, looking north. Brick was made and used in Beverley from about 1300, earlier than in most other parts of England. The more modern look of the west end (left) may therefore be misleading: such buildings appeared from the early 1400s onwards in Hull.

The ground floor dining room in the "Old Friary": the stone walls and red floor-tiles give a good impression of a late-medieval interior. The friars' refectory would have looked very similar to this, and similarly served for communal meals.

First-floor rooms provided warm, comfortable and more private quarters: this is the guests' lounge at the "Old Friary". Living upstairs became more common from the 1300s onwards. The fireplace is from a little after the friars' time.

The timber-framed roof of the upstairs "hall" appears medieval in form, and may include beams taken from the Friary ranges, if not original to this part of the building. The plaster on the east wall bears stencil-drawn floral decoration of the late 1500s or early 1600s, and traces of a garish colour-scheme of yellow and blue. The panelling is restored in 17th-century style.

Painted plaster, upstairs in the "Old Friary". This is the lesser-known of two surviving painted designs of late-medieval style. The trefoil design refers to the Holy Trinity, and is surrounded by a crown of thorns. This subject is thought by some to be associated with the friars; others believe that it records the Roman Catholic sympathies of those who occupied the building after they had been expelled.

The "Old Friary", looking south-west; a view which shows why the whole building has in the past been regarded as medieval in date. It may include materials removed from other parts of the Friary. An arch (left) covers the drain which flushed the friars' toilet. The narrow windows may come from study-cells in their dormitory.

could last between fifty and one hundred years in such a building.

From the 13th century, these posts would be set on padstones, which lifted them clear of the ground. This development may have originated with the insertion of stones to replace the rotten bases of posts set in the ground, and prevented decay at ground level. As it was no longer considered necessary to bed timbers in the ground, this indicates that more expert jointing of the superstructure could now confer extra stability on the frame. The friars' infirmary hall of about 1275, however, was built with posts bedded in the ground. This was by then an old-fashioned technique. Dark soils, left where vertical posts had rotted away, filled hollows of different sizes. An assortment of re-used timbers, which would not lend themselves to sophisticated jointing, may have been used. Alternatively, perhaps the services of a master craftsman could not be afforded. The building was to be replaced before 1320.

The rebuilt timber hall was an aisled structure. The length of roof timbers - which rarely survive on archaeological sites - between rows of posts would determine the maximum width of such a building. This internal space could be extended by the construction of aisles on either sides of the posts, with their roofs resting against the main frame. This plan-form may be seen today in churches, where stone columns take the place of the timber aisle posts.

Such a building, with a large central area and narrower spaces to the sides, was suitable for communal living. In an institutional setting, sleeping quarters or eating areas might occupy the aisles, and screens could subdivide the available space. The earlier large aisled buildings had been royal or noble halls. Like other fashions, the aisled form

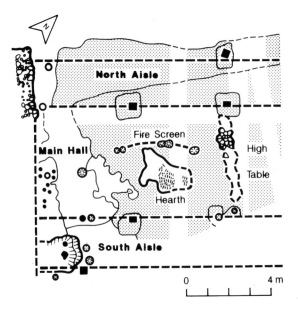

A new, aisled, hall departed from the alignment of the rest of the Friary buildings. It was perhaps an infirmary or guests' dining room. The "high end" floor (to right) may have been raised on a timber sill.

descended down the social scale in the 12th and 13th centuries, and towards the end of this period might be used by a prosperous peasant. The large open spaces within such buildings also made them useful for storage or warehousing, long after they had fallen out of favour as places to live.

Low walls in stone or brick may, despite appearances, actually represent the supports provided for horizontal timber sills. The construction of these sill-walls became increasingly common in towns from the 13th century onwards. Vertical posts would rise from, or between, the lengths of sill-beam. This method would permit the use of short lengths of wood for the sill-beams, and would protect timbers

The Tithe Barn at Easington, East Riding of Yorkshire. A rare survival of the medieval aisled building showing its timber-framed construction, and its division into "bays".

from damp, lifting them clear of the ground.

A hybrid form of construction, which may still be seen in some of the institutional buildings of York, was the construction or facing of the ground floor of a building in stone, with a timber-framed upper storey. These forms were to be widely used for residential buildings at the Beverley Priory in the 14th century, being well-adapted to the requirements of an institution with limited resources.

Timber-framed houses are warmer than those built in stone, which tend to be damp or chilly. As timber framing was a technique entailing the prefabrication of major structural elements, it also lent itself to the extension or dismantling of a building, so repairs could be carried out on one part while the rest remained in use. Such alterations were frequently undertaken in the course of the later occupation of the Priory, in response to the changing demands placed upon the friars' buildings.

In northern countries, some form of heating is necessary for any building which is to be occupied year-round. The hazards which fire presented to timber-framed buildings were obvious to medieval builders - much of Beverley, including the Minster, had been destroyed or damaged by an extensive fire in 1188. In open-plan halls, a fireplace would usually be set centrally, well away from the walls and posts. Smoke would drift up to a roof vent or louvre. Hearths could be made either from a pad of clay, which when heated would harden, or with tile fragments set on edge. In addition, small braziers might provide portable heating in cold weather. All these techniques were adopted at one time or another by the friars in the 13th century.

In the 14th century, particularly in chambers with glazed windows, the discomfort engendered by the old-fashioned central hearth encouraged the construction of wall fire-places and smoke hoods. The latter would be wicker-lined constructions daubed with plaster, to diminish the risk of fire. Where communal use of a room or other constraints made such improvements impossible, efforts were taken to screen draughts, though not always very succesfully.

As well as providing the frame of a building, timber might also be used to cover its roof, as shingles, or wooden tiles. Beverley, however, was one of the first places in England to manufacture flat roof-tiles in fired clay; they appeared in the town from the mid 12th century. The wetlands of Holderness probably also supplied abundant reed for thatching, which would have been initially cheaper, if more liable to catch fire in dry weather.

The friars' first timber hall was probably covered with thatch or shingle, though bearing a decorative crest of glazed tiles along its ridge. Their second, aisled, hall is more likely to have been roofed with red fired clay tiles, as were the majority of their later residential buildings. The variety of roof-tiles available in the town increased dramatically in the 14th century. The use of tiles, however, could involve further indirect expense through the sturdy framing of a roof capable of supporting their weight.

In summary, throughout the medieval period timber was a valuable resource, and by the 14th century it was becoming more costly. Medieval society was less inclined to wastefulness than our own, as famine and poverty were more familiar, and dangerous, to all its members. The re-use of timber was probably an integral part of the structural history of the Dominican Priory, though because the wood itself has usually rotted - or been taken away - the evidence for this is frequently indirect. The other, more durable, materials employed in the friars' buildings were frequently second-hand or of inferior quality, and the same was probably true of both the materials and the workmanship of their timber-framed residential buildings.

Flourishing Friars - The 14th Century

The 14th century was in hindsight a dangerous period, similar in many ways to our own time. Rapid population growth strained resources drawn from the farming of increasingly exhausted soils. The further loss of crops due to bad weather or epidemic diseases among livestock led to recurrent famine. England was to embark upon wars with the Scots and France, in campaigns which at first enriched, but would later impoverish the country. In the 1320s, Beverley, along with the rest of northern England, was threatened by the Scots following their victory at the battle of Bannockburn (1314).

The insecurity of 14th-century life affected all classes, and even kings could meet a violent death if they overstrained the loyalty of their more powerful noble subjects. In the middle of the century, c.1348, the Black Death, passing with trade from east to west, would wipe out one-third of a European population already weakened by hunger and war. The later part of the century would see popular revolts against secular authority and continuing schism, or division - arising from the Papacy being drawn into political conflict - in the western Church.

At the dawn of the century these apocalyptic events still lay in the future. By 1310 the Dominican community at Beverley numbered forty-two friars. This marked the high-water mark of its growth, though it was attended by difficulties, as the Prior of the Beverley house was deposed by a General Chapter of the Order in 1314.

This expansion spurred a comprehensive replanning of the friars' buildings. This was only haltingly implemented; a dependence on alms-giving imposed a brake on the rate at which work could be completed. The donation of corn to the friars in 1314,

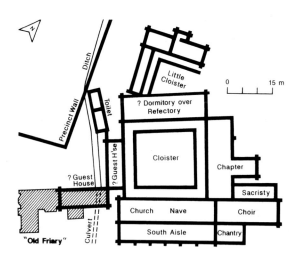

The expansion of the Friary in the 14th century - compare with the more modest layout shown on page 21. This may have followed an overall plan. However, as members of a Mendicant Order, the Beverley Dominicans could only afford to rebuild in fits and starts, as donations in cash or kind came in.

1319 and 1320, years of poor harvests, marks times where the feeding of the community may have taken precedence over projects for the improvement of its building stock.

A measure of the friars' success is provided by the addition of a south aisle to their church, probably before 1350. An arcade of piers on octagonal bases divided the nave of the original church from the new aisle, running along the course of its old south wall. This not only doubled the area available for the living to attend services, but also increased the area available for the burial of their patrons in the church.

Burial in church was, although technically illegal in canon or church law, a privilege which could be bought by a generous bequest. This assured an income for the friars, but tended to promote the idea that wealth could buy access to Heaven. This was far

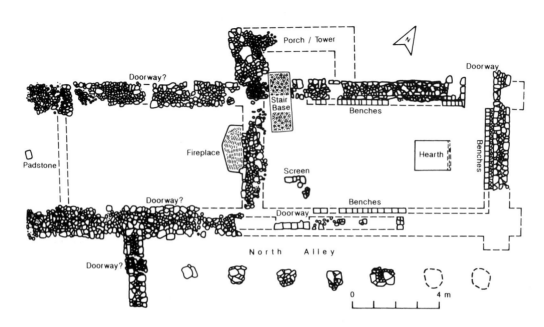

The main building of the little cloister. A communal dining room (right) replaced the facilities provided by the timber aisled hall, but more private rooms were provided at ground-floor level (left) and upstairs.

removed from the spirit in which the early mendicants had worked. The "White Lady" today resting against the wall of the "Old Friary" is an effigy formerly capping a tomb, one of the lavish memorials which multiplied in later medieval churches.

Funds made available in this way may also have contributed to other building projects. The west side of the cloister, originally of stone, was rebuilt, possibly as a partly timber-framed structure: less imposing, but more comfortable. This may have helped to extend the accommodation available within the house. Space for lay visitors was provided by the construction of a guest-house set apart from the cloister; though reconstructed, the "Old Friary" stands on earlier footings. These foundations may

have been set out at this time, as the internal width of the standing building relates it more closely to work of the early 14th century than to that of any other period.

The walling of the precinct, whose limits had hitherto been marked only by ditches or hedges, is also likely to have been undertaken in the 14th century. Such an extensive project - the enclosure of over four acres - may only have been made possible through the donation of bricks. These were manufactured nearby, along the Beverley Beck, and would be accepted as payment in kind for municipal dues, or, as here, in gift.

The aisled hall built in the 13th century was swept away. Immediately to the north of its site, a little

34

cloister was planned, perhaps to take over its function as an infirmary. Like the hall which it replaced, this lay on a different alignment to that of the church and main cloister. Its major range, to the north, was divided into two halves: a two-storey suite of private chambers to the west, and a refectory to the east. Only about twenty-two English friaries are known to have had a second cloister. Most of the others lay in the south or west of England, often in ports or other places well-placed for long-distance travel. Such extra accommodation may have housed visitors, as well as the elderly and sick of the community, and those who paid to stay there as pensioners.

The original plan for the little cloister proved overambitious. On one side, to the east, building work never advanced beyond the digging of trenches for foundations. The main, north, range was initially set out in a form which suggests that stone construction was intended throughout. Good stone was used, however, only to face that side of the building facing the rest of the monastery, and perhaps also its end wall.

The rest of the building was erected either in stone rubble, or as a timber-framed structure on rubble sill walls. Though it had glazed windows, much of the glass was of an outmoded 13th-century style, perhaps removed from the church when its south wall had been taken down in the course of its extension. A rather cramped west range was built a little later, possibly for lay-brothers, or for services ancillary to the main range. After construction in fits and starts, the little cloister was occupied by the 1320s.

If the little cloister had been laid out to anticipate the needs of a growing community, these hopes were to be disappointed. By 1335 there were only thirty friars at the Beverley Priory; a decline in numbers of a quarter over twenty-five years. The little cloister may, however, have helped to meet extraordinary demands on accommodation. One such event would have been a further Provincial Chapter of the English Dominicans, which was held in Beverley in 1342.

Though the impact of the Black Death on the Priory is unknown, it can hardly have swelled income or the number of friars. Houses with spare capacity would put it to varied uses. One was the settlement of corrodians, or pensioners, whose places would depend on a donation to cover the cost of their keep. In 1356, Roger de Querndon, a royal chaplain "broken with age", was retired to Beverley at royal expense; he may have lived out his last days in the little cloister.

By the 15th century, and possibly before that time if space were available, the Prior might also have had a separate lodging there. Important visitors, or those in Holy Orders, may have been put up here as his guests. They included travellers from far afield: coins from Scotland and the continent, and glassware perhaps from Venice, were found here. Further works on the little cloister in the course of the 14th century were intended to enhance the comfort of its communal areas, and to increase the private accommodation available.

Though privacy and comfort are signs of progress in a secular world, they may detract from a communal religious life of simplicity and prayer. This problem appears to have been addressed in the later 14th century, by the renewal of buildings which figured in the communal life of the Priory. Although this implies a degree of local prosperity, presumably a generation or so after the Black Death, it also required energetic fund-raising. Chaucer, based at Court in Westminster, may have heard of this. He perhaps had Beverley in mind when writing the

Canterbury Tales in the 1380s; this is the opening of the Summoner's Tale:

"My lords, there lies - in Yorkshire as I guess -
A marshy district known as Holderness,
In which a friar, a limiter [preacher], went about
To preach his sermons and to beg, no doubt.
And on a certain day it so befell,
When he had preached in church, and cast his spell
With one main object, far above the rest,
To fire his congregation with a zest
For buying trentals, and for Jesu's sake
To give the wherewithall for friars to make
Their holy houses..."

The Beverley Dominicans and Franciscans were the only Mendicant communities in Holderness, and it is significant that a building programme figures in what develops as an uncomplimentary tale of extortion. It is possible that the choir of the Dominican church was enlarged about this time.

It is certain that the main cloister saw a dramatic expansion. It was shifted northwards, so that the old back (north) wall of its north range became the south wall of a large new refectory built in stone. This may have had a dormitory above it, as the toilet block was also extended northwards, to maintain access between these buildings. The dormitory would be divided into study-bedrooms, each with a small window to admit light so that each friar could work in his room. It was usual to have the friars' library at one end of the dormitory, so the books would be available to those engaged in academic work.

This extension of the main cloister effected a junction with the little cloister. The latter was partially rebuilt and drains laid, to prevent its lawn or garth - the open space enclosed by its buildings - from being flooded by rainwater running off the roofs of the enlarged complex. The rebuilding here employed techniques associated with timber-framed construction, so comfort would have been more important than display in the little cloister. The buildings of the Priory had almost achieved their maximum extent by 1400. This, however, may have been at the expense of popular tolerance for the friars, whose professed poverty contrasted with the scale and comfort of their dwellings.

The Friary in the first half of the 15th century.

1: Choir - Shown here as it may have been rebuilt by c.1390; this was the private part of the church where the round of "Offices" was observed. The tower and spire are conjectural, based on an illustration of Norwich Blackfriars. On the north side of the choir is the sacristy - the priest's changing room.

2: Chantry Chapel - Containing at least one tomb, this was perhaps built originally for a member of the Holme family buried in the later 1300s. Masses would be bought, and sung here for their personal benefit.

3: Preaching Nave - The part of the church open to the public, and where other rich patrons would be buried.

4: Nave Extension (or south aisle) - Added in the early 1300s, to double the public area of the church used by the living, and to make room for more tombs.

5: Guesthouse - Perhaps built in the early 1300s, this now lies under the stone-built end of the "Old Friary".

6: Kitchen - Rebuilt in the early 1300s, perhaps with accomodation upstairs.

7: North Range - Rebuilt in the late 1300s, with a refectory downstairs; the dormitory with its study cells is thought to have been upstairs. It was probably this building that was damaged in 1449, when the friars' library was lost in a fire.

8: Toilet - Flushed by a "common sewer". Built in the 1200s, this was extended when (7) was built, to maintain access to it from the dormitory.

9: Great Cloister - The covered alleys linked various parts of the Friary. A cistern in the middle was filled by a piped water supply. Water was distributed from here by gravity to other parts of the complex.

10: Chapter House - Projecting back from the east range, this was a "Parliament" for the friars, where they regulated their affairs in regular meetings.

11: Little Cloister - Built in the early 1300s, it had achieved this form by c.1400. A dining room for guests and elderly friars, lit by a large window, lies at one end, with more private apartments at the other. It is linked to the main cloister by a narrow building which may have housed lay-brothers or servants.

12: Fish Ponds - Lying to the north of the buildings of the Friary, these contributed to a partially abstinent diet. Other closes included orchards, gardens and pasture, which helped supply the community.

13: Precinct Wall - Built in brick in the 1300s, with later gateways, to enhance the privacy of the Friary.

Stone and Brick in the Priory Buildings

The construction of buildings in stone has always carried a strong symbolic charge, conveying notions of stability and permanence. In Beverley, an area devoid of good building stone, it also signified the wealth or prestige of those who could afford it.

The nearest suitable stones for building were the Oolitic Limestones which outcrop near North and South Cave, among other places, on the Yorkshire Wolds. These were extensively quarried until the later 12th century. Thereafter, paler Magnesian Limestones from Tadcaster and Doncaster, brought by river to Beverley, formed the most usual raw material for stone masons working in the town. Beverley Minster is mostly constructed of Tadcaster limestone, with decorative internal black "marble" shafts coming all the way from Purbeck, on the Isle of Wight. The Magnesian Limestones are finely grained, and permitted more delicate decorative carving of window and door frames than was possible with the Cave stone.

The scarcity of stone encouraged the re-use of material stripped from redundant or modernised structures. Work on the rebuilding of Beverley Minster through the 13th century left fragments of its older fabric on almost every nearby medieval site. The friars re-used this stone to mend or modify their own buildings; it often bears diagonal tool-marks or other decorative features which betray its origin in earlier structures of 12th-century date.

Given the expense of stone, its use by the friars was initially reserved for buildings with a particular ritual importance, such as the church, or those parts of the cloister where they passed some part of the regulated life. Their use of stone almost invariably signalled the importance of the structures in which it appeared.

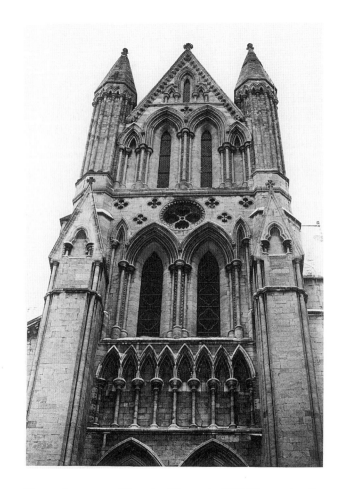

The south transept of Beverley Minster, in 1997. The construction of the present building began about 1220, and it was rising amid scaffolding when the Dominican friars arrived at Beverley. Their first stone buildings were constructed in a similar Early English style, but were plainer and on a more modest scale.

The friars' first stone buildings would have been in the Early English or Transitional style, though executed on a much more modest scale than appears at Beverley Minster.

The proximity of the Minster was useful to the friars because its reconstruction meant that large numbers of masons would have been working in the town. The skill of masons lay not merely in the working of stone, but also in surveying, architecture and design. It has been suggested above that a professional hand is discernible in the initial planning of the friars' cloister.

It seems that 13th-century stone buildings at the Priory may have been laid out in units of half-perches - in the pre-decimal system of measurement, a perch was sixteen and a half feet - the perch was widely used as a unit of land measurement. Later buildings were planned by reference to the dimensions of existing ones. This seems to have been done most carefully when buildings played an important part in the regulated life of the community -the later 14th-century refectory is an example.

It is possible that the 14th-century addition of an aisle to the church, and work at its east end, was planned according to length-to-width ratios of six-to-one and three-to-one respectively. The evidence from Beverley is inconclusive on this point, though such proportions have been recorded for other later mendicant churches, and these aspects of design may have related to a widespread contemporary interest in the Holy Trinity. The form of the church choir could reflect that of God, whose house it was!

The design of the main range of the little cloister is strikingly similar to that of an equivalent structure at the Franciscan Priory in Carmarthen. Here, the use of a "standard" plan may suggest that its design was taken from a copy-book - effectively a catalogue, which a master mason would show to his clients. While timber buildings would usually be erected according to local conventions, masons were well-travelled professionals, and their work could draw on practice or innovation from far afield.

Stone walls required firm foundations, especially where, as at the Priory, the ground was soft and damp. Building work was preceded by landscaping, involving the movement of tons of soil, or the laying down of thick rafts of clay. Footing trenches were then dug, their depth depending on local ground conditions. They were filled either with pitched chalk rubble or roughly coursed blocks, again according to the nature of the ground. Chalk was available locally on the Westwood, and was used in massive quantities in medieval Beverley, for building footings and, from the 14th century, for the paving of important streets.

Such foundations tended to draw in water, acting like land-drains, and so were sealed with clay to prevent it springing up through them. A bed of mortar then prepared the surface of the footing for the construction of the wall above it; fragments of flat-laid tile helped do this, and also levelled courses of walls built of stones of slightly different sizes.

The footing was usually wider than the wall above it; stone walls intended to rise to a height of two storeys, or for larger buildings, were at least one metre or three feet wide. Single-storey or sill walls were a little over half this thickness. Walls might also be slightly thickened if they were to be interrupted by large windows. The blocks of freestone, so called because it could be freely cut into rectangular shapes, were then laid in regular courses. The outer faces of the blocks were smooth, but irregularities on the faces built into the wall usefully trapped the lime mortar used to bond them together.

As with their timber-framed structures, the friars' stone buildings betray a somewhat old-fashioned approach dictated by the indifferent quality of the materials available to them. Throughout the Dominican occupation, stone walls were constructed with an outer "skin" of limestone, a rubble core, and an inner "skin" of chalk. The chalk would have to be sheltered from weathering, as frost could rapidly shatter it. These methods were usual in the 12th and 13th centuries. From the later 14th century, however, construction with larger blocks of stone making up the full thickness of a wall was favoured. The friars were unable to keep up with fashion in this respect, and later stone buildings at the Priory were less finely finished than their predecessors. The old technique permitted smaller, second-hand, blocks to be used.

The main cloister north range wall, with an outer face of limestone (foreground), an inner face of chalk, and a rubble core between them.

Windows and doors gave opportunities for decoratively carved stonework. The Dominicans' Constitutions forbade excessive ornamentation of their buildings, which would in any case have been impractically costly. A few fragments of carved stone from window frames have been recovered, mostly of the Decorated style favoured in the later 14th century. The curvilinear form of these frames may have been repeated in the painted decoration of the window glass which they enclosed, though, unlike richer houses, this was mostly monochrome rather than coloured. These window frames were less ornate than those in contemporary monasteries which did not share the mendicant ideal. Doorways were also plain.

A fireplace built in the little cloister in the early 14th century was originally flanked with decorative columns. These, however, were put together with reclaimed stone, and were painted so as to imitate the more expensive Purbeck "marble" shafts which still remain within Beverley Minster. These features were later dismantled, perhaps because of structural failure, or because such ostentation was regarded as unseemly by a later generation of friars.

The cost of building in stone restricted its use. The main range of the 14th-century little cloister, however, seems to have been erected with some pretensions to status. The ground-floor wall of the building facing the rest of the monastery was built of smooth pale limestone. Its back wall, however, was of coursed rubble, perhaps only serving as a sill to support a timber frame. The building thus presented its best face to the rest of the community's buildings, and its less impressive aspect to the gardens and ponds behind. Thus, the facade of a stone building may have masked a more comfortable timber-framed house.

The first-floor apartments in the little cloister were probably timber-framed. The plastering of irregular stonework, or of timber-framed buildings, could help them blend in with more costly masonry structures: this deceptive technique was also used in the 14th century when the west range of the main cloister was rebuilt.

Because of the local dearth of stone, and an increasing scarcity of timber, the use of brick as a building material was resorted to earlier in this region

Wall of the main cloister west range, showing the stone and brick of three distinct periods of work. These were revealed by the removal of a cosmetic plaster coating which was added to tidy up after the last phase of rebuilding.

The little cloister north range wall: similar, but narrower. A bench-footing made of re-used tiles (centre) is set against the wall.

than in many other places. Brick was widely available in 14th-century Beverley, while the medieval walls of Hull have been calculated to have included 4.8 million bricks. As brick was manufactured along the Beverley Beck, the friars may have received surplus bricks as donations from manufacturers - sometimes these were of low quality, perhaps not good enough to be sold.

In the 14th century, brick was used for fixtures and fittings within buildings: drain conduits or bench-footings. It might also infill the panels of a timber-framed building, set herring-bone fashion rather than in horizontal courses, as can still be observed in the outer wall of the Tap and Spile public house (formerly the Sun Inn), near the end of Friars Lane.

In the later 14th century, brick came to be used with greater confidence. It served in sill walls, and eventually for upstanding walling as is familiar today. The brick wall around the friars' precinct was probably built in the later 14th century. Its lower, thicker, part was of the same "hollow" construction as was used for building in stone, but its upper extent

West | East

Brick

Chalk

Mortar

0   1 m

A view through the 14th-century precinct boundary, showing the (then) "modern-style" brick wall supported by a footing built like an "old fashioned" stone wall.

was solid coursed brickwork. So, too, were walls which ran across the precinct to meet it. A small chantry chapel attached to the east end of the church was built entirely of brick in the late 14th or 15th century. The "Old Friary" is of brick at one end, probably work of the 15th or 16th century, though raised on the footings of an earlier building at the other.

The roofs of stone buildings would normally be framed in timber, and their roofs would be clad in the same way as those of wooden buildings, often with tiles. For the most important structures, lead sheet may have been used, as is still traditional today for church roofs. Lead roofs require renewal only about once a century, so maintenance costs would be low, though the initial outlay was formidable. Lead sheet was rolled and sealed to form piping to bring fresh water into the monastery. It had other uses, usually in the sealing of drains and gutters, though was used sparingly because of its cost.

Lead was also used to frame small panes of glass, which would be pieced together like a jig-saw to form sheets of glazing for windows. These were again expensive, and would initially be provided only in the church, and perhaps the chapter house. Renewal of these windows would permit old glass to be used elsewhere to enhance the comfort of residential quarters.

The ruins of monasteries in remote locations give an impression of the ambitious scope of projects undertaken by medieval masons, and a weathered impression of the rich ornamentation which it was possible to render in stone. The decoration and scale of the friars' urban houses was altogether more modest. This predominantly undecorated stonework lent itself to re-use, particularly in areas where natural resources were limited. The physical remains of friars' houses are correspondingly rare, at least above ground.

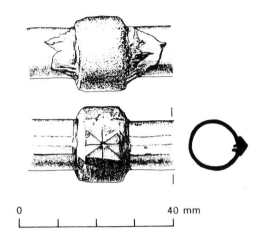

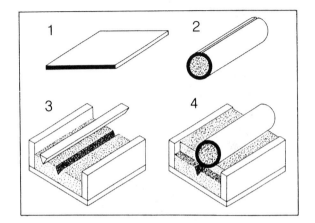

0   40 mm

Above left: A lead pipe excavated from the Friary in 1963, featuring the collar joining two lengths, bearing the plumbers mark. The diagram on the right shows the stages of making waterpipes: casting a sheet of lead 5mm thick (1); wrapping it around a wooden mandrel or former of 50mm diameter and filling the tube with sand (2); pressing a wooden fillet into a sand bed to form a trough (3); and laying the sand-filled tube with its seam over the trough, into which molten lead is poured to seal the seam (4). Once the casting had cooled, the sand would be cleaned out, leaving a watertight length of pipe.

The Later Years - the Friars in the 15th Century

The disasters of the 14th century were to bear fruit in following years. Merchants had begun to usurp the dynamic role of traditional authorities in national affairs; locally, Hull's commercial success was at the expense of older towns such as Beverley. This development was encouraged locally by royal patronage of Kingston upon Hull, which had been favoured over Beverley from the 1320s onwards.

The prestige of the aristocracy declined as the English foothold in France was whittled away, and ancient lines of noble descent died out - often from a failure to produce heirs, rather than through battle. Discharged soldiers took to banditry or swelled noble retinues competing for control of the Crown. When the strife between the houses of York and Lancaster ended with Henry VII's accession in 1485, political power was concentrated in royal hands. From this time onwards the Crown was to enjoy the support of Parliaments which upheld the status quo, and which were to come to represent the interests of the rich and newly respectable.

In 1400, criticism of the Church by the Lollards, or "babblers", had been suppressed by royal order. The subsequent failure to address abuses such as the marketing of religious services, weakened respect for the Church. While the interests of religious and secular authorities coincided, the Crown continued to uphold the established order. The invention of printing in the 15th century meant that books, which had formerly been copied by hand, became more widely available. Increasing numbers of people could read the Bible and other works for themselves, without requiring a religious intermediary.

The weakening of the mendicant ideal in the later Middle Ages had forced modification of the fund-raising expedients upon which the friars depended. Reliance upon daily alms-giving gave way to longer-term arrangements with benefactors. Where there was space to spare, elderly patrons or others would be taken in to live with the friars, their keep being payed for by a down-payment, or by a regular allowance. This could prove expensive if the guest lived to a ripe old age.

More profit could be gleaned from offering mortuary services: the sale of burial space in friars' churches, and of Chantry Masses recited for the repose of the souls of patrons. Families might maintain a connection with the house over generations. In 1309, Thomas, son of Alexander de Holme, had proposed to grant land to the Beverley Dominicans. In 1421 John, son of Richard de Holme, was buried in the church, and by 1448 it contained the Holme Altar. Either this or another foundation was supported by rents still held by the Priory in 1539. A brick-built chapel used for burial was attached to the east end of the nave of the church, and may date to this period.

Along with services to benefactors, living or dead, links were also strengthened with local institutions serving workers and tradesmen in Beverley. During disputes in the later 14th century, the Dominicans had served as neutral custodians of the town chest, receiving six shillings for their services. In 1414 the tailors of Beverley assembled in the friars' gardens for their annual Guild meeting. By 1493, the Porters and Creelers (or basket-men) of the town also held an annual procession at the friars' church on the first Sunday after the feast of the Assumption. The Guild of St Peter of Milan was a devotional organisation in the town, named after a Dominican martyred in Italy, and linked to the Priory. A "Galilee" porch was attached to the west end of the church in the 14th century or later, and figured in processions or meetings in which lay-people took an important part.

The last archaeological evidence for occupation in the little cloister is dated to the mid 15th century. This was not followed by its abandonment, but rather by an end to activity at ground-floor level, most significantly in the little cloister refectory. This suggests that attempts to revive communal life were flagging by this time. Similarly, the austerities of diet and discipline which had distinguished friars from other monks in the 13th century had been eroded. The friars were repeatedly singled out for criticism by their contemporaries in the later 14th century. Both literary and archaeological evidence confirm that many aspects of the Dominican Constitutions had fallen quietly into abeyance by the later medieval period.

The latest structural alterations in the little cloister related to the provision of stairs and facilities - perhaps including a fireplace - to improve the private apartments upstairs. Ground-floor rooms served only to give access to those above, or for storage. It may also be surmised that accommodation in the main cloister was at first-floor level by this time. An accidental fire in the friars' library, which was usually housed at one end of the dormitory, led to a royal grant of ten marks to defray the expenses of repairs in 1449. As noted above, this dormitory had probably been constructed at first-floor level in the late 14th century, above the refectory. These developments hint at a more private and comfortable way of life than had been envisaged by the founders of the Mendicant Orders.

Dead Patrons Pay - Burial at the Dominican Priory

The medieval preoccupation with death and the hereafter is readily explained by the insecurity of life at the time. The lack of sanitation and medical services, the resultant prevalence of disease, and the intermittent threat of famine, left living conditions precarious. The Church promoted Christian values through the incentive of eternal life-after-death in Heaven for the virtuous, or the threat of eternal torment for sinners.

Mystery Plays conveyed religious teaching to a largely illiterate audience, and would be presented by religious fellowships and guilds. Hell was a popular subject, not least because it called for the latest special effects!

Some moderation of the abuses committed by the powerful could be imposed by playing on their fear of Divine Judgement, while the rebellious tendencies of the oppressed could similarly be discouraged. Churchmen could also set an example of generosity or humility, to be followed by those in authority. The passage of an individual from this world to the next, and their arrival in Heaven, could be eased by prayer offered on his or her behalf. This would naturally be most effective if prayers were offered by a member of a religious Order, whose life was dedicated to continual communication with God.

It was obvious to the medieval mind that the nearer the body was buried to a place of regular prayer, the more benefit the soul which had inhabited the body would gain from that prayer. Virtue could be gained by association, particularly with the remains of holy people, or with holy places. Throughout the medieval period, and in defiance of ecclesiastical law, burial in a church offered the prospect of benefits which were quite literally out of this world.

In the later Middle Ages, prayers sung for the souls of named individuals - Chantry Masses - were regarded as especially effective, and priests might be employed solely for this purpose. Both burial space and prayer had come to be marketable commodities; offered in return for donations or bequests. The attractions of such an exchange to the friars, who had excluded themselves from profitable enterprise, and yet had communities to maintain, were clear. There was a general consensus on the value of such arrangements up to the later 14th century: contemporary criticism centred on the failure to offer prayers which had been purchased, rather than on the marketing of spiritual services.

Burials have been recorded in several locations within the Beverley Priory. There were conventions as to who could be buried where, and possibly as to the form that the burial might take. Certain rules were widely applied: burial with the head to the west was customary for all except priests. This ancient custom was rationalised as facing the east, where the sun rises, and whence Christ would return to the world at the Last Judgement - priests were sometimes buried the other way round so that they would face the congregation when they rose from the grave. The body would be laid on its back, often with hands or arms folded; this posture might be cramped if a wooden coffin were used, which appears to have been usual for those lay people who could afford it.

An ordinary friar would usually be buried under the alley of the main cloister, probably unclothed or shrouded. The body was simply being lowered into the grave and laid in an extended position. All those burials recorded in the cloister were adult males, and were buried without coffins. The use of the alley for burial forbade the erection of memorial markers, which would impede passage along it by the living. The friar would therefore remain an anonymous part of his community, and in keeping with holy humility would rest literally under the feet of subsequent generations of friars. The limitations on available space meant that up to three tiers of graves eventually lay along some alleys; the greatest numbers have been recorded on the west side of the cloister.

In other monasteries, as at the Augustinian friars' house in Hull, it appears that young people - perhaps choirboys or novices studying to become friars - were buried in particular parts of the alley. On occasion, patrons of the Beverley house would also request burial in the cloister, perhaps so they could in death join a community which they had supported during their lifetime. Thus, John of Hessle was buried there next to his wife Beatrice, in 1349.

The Prior of the house would by custom be buried in the choir of the friars' church; at Beverley, probably before the high altar. The tiles on the floor of the church would be lifted to permit this. Most graves in the choir bore no surviving signs of markers. One, however, took the form of a brick-lined chamber, and this may have been covered by a more visible memorial slab. Particularly important patrons might occasionally be granted the honour of burial here. So, too, were members of noble or even royal families killed in times of political turmoil. Richard III was laid to rest in the Leicester Franciscans' church after his death at the battle of Bosworth in 1485. Henry Tudor, who took the throne as Henry VII, would not have wished to dignify his defeated rival with a state funeral at Westminster Abbey.

The nave of the friars' church, and from the 14th century its aisle, saw the burial of lay people who had purchased an association with the Priory. The examination of skeletons excavated here shows that they included the remains of men, women and young people. Wills sometimes specified where in the church people wished to be buried. In 1428 Thomas Hilton requested burial just inside the south door of the church, while in 1476 William Horn asked to be buried before the image of St Mary in the centre of the nave. Graves in the nave and aisle usually contained a coffined body. The coffin would be constructed of wooden planks, and was sometimes packed with grass or straw, perhaps to prevent the body rolling about on its way to the grave.

Excavations in Hull have shown that later medieval practice sometimes favoured clothed burial; there, exceptionally damp conditions have led to the survival of fragments of garments. The dead person might be portrayed as an effigy on top of their grave, usually clothed, and sometimes as a recognisable portrait. The "White Lady" is a slab from on top of a 14th-century woman's grave, now resting against the wall of the "Old Friary". Such sculpture would emphasise the wealth of those who could afford it, and niches and canopies might be erected over the graves of the richest - the Percy Tomb in Beverley Minster is an example of the most sumptuous style of later medieval monument. The friars also had a churchyard where space could be found for the burial of those of more modest means.

The profitability of these arrangements seems to have peaked between 1390 and 1410 for the Beverley Dominicans, to judge from bequests recorded in their favour. At this time, or shortly after, a small chapel built in brick was added to the east end of the aisle. This contained a large brick-lined tomb. This may have lain before the Holme Altar, recorded in 1448. The tomb was for a member or members of a family who were important patrons of the house.

If patrons could afford the construction of a chapel, they would also have made financial arrangements for regular prayers or Chantry Masses to be recited. Such an investment represented an insurance policy taken out by someone whose busy life or profitable business may have led them to neglect spiritual matters. The visible decoration of a tomb or chapel also underlined the influence of the family which maintained it for all to see.

These arrangements were dependent on the ability of the friars to keep up the round of prayers to which they were contracted. Irregularity within a monastery detracted from the market-value of the services it offered. The Catholic belief that salvation depended solely upon Divine Grace, dispensed by the Church, was challenged by a notion later associated with Protestantism: that salvation depended on good works. The medieval writer Langland, a cleric writing in the later 14th century, expressed this in his

Left: A coffined burial laid in a brick-lined tomb, from the Augustinian Friary in Hull. Right: A monument from above a similar tomb in the church of the Beverley Dominican Friary. This now rests against the wall of the "Old Friary", and is known as the "White Lady".

allegorical work Piers Ploughman, in which the character "Do Well" was contrasted with others, including friars, who personified various vices.

Langland did not challenge the authority of the Church, but rather the failings of its servants. Later generations brought a more sceptical eye to bear on the practices which it permitted. At the Reformation, chantries established with the intention of securing perpetual prayer on the behalf of wealthy founders were obvious targets for suppression.

The Fading of an Ideal - The Decline of the Priory and the Dissolution of the Monasteries

The Renaissance, though coming late to England, was to encourage a critical examination of established institutions which they were ill-equipped to withstand. For the Church, this paved the way for the movement which became known as the Reformation. When Henry VIII broke with the Papacy over his plans for remarriage, he would harness first the movement for religious reform, and then the greed of new monied classes, to assist his Dissolution of the monasteries of England.

The royal grant of 1449, following the destruction of their library, had referred to the friars' poverty. This may have been a polite formula to justify an appeal for royal funds. A legal action for the recovery of debt from one of the Beverley friars in 1434, however, may show that they were facing genuine and longstanding financial difficulties. By the late 15th century there were only fourteen friars resident in the house. The silence of the historical record hints that these circumstances had taken their toll by the early 16th century: between 1505 and 1520 no bequests to the friars are recorded.

A grant made before 1525, admitting Lord Darcy as a sort of honorary friar - and perhaps booking his place as a pensioner, claimed that his assistance had rescued a monastery which was dilapidated (the term literally means stripped of stone) and non-functional. Though this may overstate the true position, it confirms that the Priory had passed through a difficult period.

From 1520 until the Dissolution of the house in 1539, bequests in favour of the Dominicans are again recorded. They were in a better state than many other houses. The friars were still the sole occupants of the Priory at the Dissolution; Beverley's Franciscan monastery had been letting rooms as holiday flats for years, and elsewhere retired folk or families were well-established in monastic precincts.

There were attempts to revive the mendicant ideal at the end of the medieval period; Observant friars aspired to observe the early rigorous standards of austerity, and had founded or reformed several English houses by the early years of the 16th century. It is possible that Lord Darcy's assistance had been intended to permit such a rejuvenation of the Dominican Priory at Beverley.

The reforming movement was, however, overtaken by Henry VIII's dispute with the Pope, and his assumption of leadership of the Church of England. The Dissolution of the monasteries made this step irrevocable. The Pilgrimage of Grace, a popular revolt against this policy in the north of England, saw rebels assemble in arms at Beverley in October 1536, and again in 1537. There was widespread local sympathy for their cause. The "Pilgrims" marched on Hull, which fell to them despite its defensive walls. The dispersal of the rebels, and the failure of a second rising, saw the reassertion of royal authority with widespread executions. This repression set the seal on the seizure and sale of Church property, which amounted to nearly one-third of the kingdom.

The expulsion of the friars was the responsibility of Royal Commissioners, who travelled the country to survey and secure their property and, if they cooperated, to set pensions for those displaced. One described his work as follows: "I pulled down no house thoroughly at none of the Friars, but so defaced them as they should not lightly be made Friaries again". The turn of the Beverley Dominicans came in 1539. The eviction of the friars was followed by asset-stripping which was intended to prevent

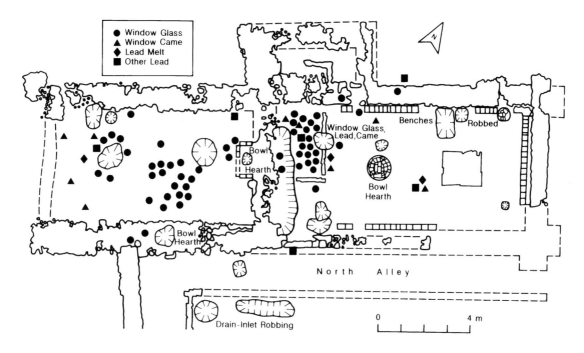

Legend:
- ● Window Glass
- ▲ Window Came
- ◆ Lead Melt
- ■ Other Lead

Asset-stripping: The very detailed evidence for the looting of the little cloister north range at the Dissolution of the Friary. The scattered fragments of broken-up windows surround the hearths where their lead cames were melted down.

their return, though the shells of some buildings stood empty afterwards, or were put to new uses. The land of the Beverley Priory was surveyed and initially leased; in 1544 it was bought up by property speculators based in London along with a mass of other "privatised" religious holdings.

The main cloister of the Beverley Dominicans was torn down. Rubbish flung into the toilet was dated to the early decades of the 16th century, necessarily marking the end of ordered occupation in the building which it served. Material robbed from the cloister may have been piled in its garth; building stone was a precious commodity in Beverley, and the best may have rapidly been re-used. Lead pipes were

withdrawn from their conduits, at least where their whereabouts were known. Tiled floors in the church were lifted and removed.

The wrecking of the little cloister has been investigated in greater detail, and gives a more exact impression of what this process involved. Material from the latest occupation of the ranges was flung out into the garth. Within buildings, fixtures were dismantled. Windows were bodily removed, those at first-floor level being flung downstairs, where a tangle of glass set in lead piled up in the stairwell. This was then broken up; better glass was perhaps recovered, the lead being melted down in bowl-shaped hearths in the ground-floor rooms.

The "Old Friary" as its restoration began - an image which may give an impression of the last days of the little cloister - only the car betrays a recent date!

The location of the bowl-hearths indicates that this procedure was followed room by room. Some were cut into existing fireplaces. Where a fireplace was not available, a new hearth was constructed with bricks displaced from bench-footings, and was perhaps fuelled with wood from the benches. While work continued, hearths were plugged with clay between periods of use to avoid accidental fire. The last of the hearths lay in a doorway, and was left open, suggesting both that inflammable fittings had been removed, and that access to the shell of the building was no longer required.

Roofs were stripped of tiles; as only broken roof-tiles were left behind in the garth in modest quantities, these were presumably re-used. If tile was worth reclaiming, it is certain that roof timbers would also

have been taken and timber frames disassembled. Down-pipes and gutters were also pulled off or dug out. The extent of stone-robbing is uncertain here, though internal walls seem to have been brought down. The final robbing of stone from the walls of the little cloister north range was dated to the 17th or 18th century, so ruins may have survived until that time.

The date of the standing building known as the "Old Friary" is uncertain. Excavations within and around the building suggest that it represents a late addition, though one raised on the pre-existing footings of a building of medieval date. Though doorways and the stone-built eastern end of the "Old Friary" are medieval in style, they may show the reuse of materials. This could have taken place during the last

52

difficult stages of the Dominican occupation, or immediately after its close. The use of this part of the precinct for guests, rather than for monastic purposes, may have permitted it to be left undamaged at the Dissolution.

Alternatively, the "Old Friary" may have been constructed with stone robbed from other buildings of the Priory at their demolition. The wall-paintings at its western, brick-built, end could plausibly be associated with the Dominican occupation. They could equally mark the private devotional interest of lay-folk; Catholic sympathies were widespread in Beverley, and public conformity with the Church of England was usually the most that the Tudor state required of tender consciences.

Design from the painted wall-plaster upstairs in the "Old Friary". The blackbirds may be a visual reference to the Blackfriars. The text reads either "Jesu Mercy" or "Ave Maria"; both readings could suggest Roman Catholic devotion. This painting, however, could date to either before or after the Dissolution.

Suggestions for Further Reading

A wealth of recent studies of the history and archaeology of Beverley are available. For research, volumes published by the Royal Commission for Historic Monuments, with a bias towards buildings (Miller et al. 1983), and by the Victoria County History, dealing with documentary sources (Allison 1989), are indispensable. A regional overview is provided by Neave and Ellis (1996). The Sites and Monuments Record maintained by the Humber Archaeology Partnership includes a cumulative record of site-specific information for East Yorkshire. The Public Libraries in Beverley and Hull also hold local history collections.

A few standard works consider the history and remains of the Mendicant Orders in England; most are available on order from larger libraries. Hinnebusch (1951) deals with the Dominicans; Martin with particular houses (1929; 1935) and with the Franciscans (1937); and Roth (1966) with the Augustinians. Archaeological study of the Mendicant Orders has been reviewed by Butler (1984).

Archaeological reports provide detailed analysis of sites at the south end of Beverley and the finds excavated from them. These deal with the Dominican Priory itself (Armstrong and Tomlinson 1987; Foreman 1996); the friars' neighbours on Eastgate (Evans and Tomlinson 1992); and the Anglo-Saxon monastery of St John and its medieval successors (Armstrong et al. 1991). They are copiously illustrated, include accessible summaries and discussions, and present the full range of evidence available from excavations, together with extensive bibliographies. The annual publications of the East Riding Archaeological Society, and the Yorkshire Archaeological Journal, continue to present the results of past and on-going research into the history of the region.

For background reading, English Heritage and Batsford have produced a range of titles which present thematic and period-based studies drawing on fieldwork in England. The Shire series of pocket-sized volumes also presents reliable topical studies. Hutton Press presents similarly convenient titles for East Yorkshire. Those teaching in schools should also be aware of display panels and booklets presenting period-based views of the region's archaeology, which draw upon recent work. These are available from the Humber Archaeology Partnership.

The later-medieval friar at work in his study cell, which was a sort of study bedroom. Books were kept in a library at one end of the dormitory.

Bibliography

Allison, K.J. (ed.) 1989
A History of the County of York, East Riding. Vol. 6: The Borough and Liberties of Beverley (V.C.H.), London.

Armstrong, P. and Tomlinson, D.G. 1987
Excavations at the Dominican Priory, Beverley, 1960-1983, Humberside Heritage Publ. 13, Humberside Leisure Services, Hull.

Armstrong, P., Tomlinson, D.G. and Evans, D.H. 1991
Excavations at Lurk Lane, Beverley 1979-1982, Sheffield Excavation Report 1.

Butler, L.A.S. 1984
The Houses of the Mendicant Orders in Britain: Recent Archaeological Work, in Addyman, P.V. and Black, V.E. (eds), Archaeological papers from York presented to M.W. Barley, York Archaeological Trust, 123-36.

Evans, D.H. and Tomlinson, D.G. 1992
Excavations at 33-35 Eastgate, Beverley 1983-1986, Sheffield Excavation Report 3.

Foreman, M. 1996
Further Excavations at the Dominican Priory, Beverley, 1986-1989, Sheffield Excavation Report 4.

Hinnebusch, W.A. 1951
The Early English Friars Preachers, Institutum Historicum FF. Praedicatorum Romae AD S. Sabinae, Dissertationes Historicae Fasciculus XIV, Rome.

Martin, A.R. 1929
The Dominican Priory at Canterbury, Archaeol. J. 86 (1929), 152-77.

Martin, A.R. 1935
The Grey Friars of Walsingham, Norfolk Archaeol. 25 (1935), 227-71.

Martin, A.R. 1937
Franciscan Architecture in England, Brit. Soc. Franciscan Studies 18 (for 1933-34), Manchester: University Press.

Miller, K.;Robinson, J; English, B. and Hall, I. 1982
Beverley: An Archaeological and Architectural Study, Royal Comm. Hist. Mons. England, Suppl. Ser. 4, London, HMSO.

Neave, S. and Ellis, S. (eds) 1996
An Historical Atlas of East Yorkshire, Hull, University of Hull Press.

Roth, F. 1966
The English Austin Friars 1249-1538. Vol. 1: History, New York.

Acknowledgements

Our thanks go out to the many workers - from local trainees or amateur archaeologists to renowned academics - who have quite literally brought hitherto unwritten stories to the light of day at Beverley Friary. Their efforts span the four decades from 1960 to 1996. Though there is not space to list them here - their names may be found in many of the works listed above - we owe to their energies and dedication all that is presented here. It is the view of this author, a view shared by many of those involved in successive seasons of fieldwork, that if one individual were to be thanked as standing for all, that person would be Peter Armstrong, formerly Field Officer for the Humberside Archaeology Unit (HAU).

Although archaeologists may sometimes feel an uncomfortable degree of kinship with the Mendicant Orders whose lives have been explored here, the agencies which have had the wisdom and foresight to support their labours with public funds also deserve recognition. They include English Heritage, the Manpower Services Commission, Beverley Workbridge, the former Beverley Borough and Humberside County Councils, and their successors in local government, the East Riding of Yorkshire and Hull City Councils. Many other bodies and private individuals have also made their own timely contributions; once again, they are named elsewhere.

Graphics in this book are principally the work of Mike Frankland; in some cases adapted from the publications of HAU. Further drawings are by Karen Guffog (Page 5), Elizabeth Hall (Page 56), Peter Harrison (Page 45), Linda Smith (Page 24), and Bryda Robins (Pages 8 and 43). Line drawings from medieval manuscripts were redrawn from collections published by D. Hartley and M. Elliot in the 1930s, as Life and Work of the People of England (vol. 2). Excavation photographs are drawn from HAU archives held by the Hull and East Riding Museum, while colour plates and other photographs were taken by Les Gibbon (Pages 27-29, and 48) and Gail Foreman (Page 38).

Sister Mary Josephine, of the Poor Clares Monastery at Lynton, North Devon, is warmly thanked for her valuable first-hand comment on daily life in a Mendicant house. Advice from Dave Evans, who has kindly read earlier texts and made many constructive suggestions for their improvement, and the patient assistance of Ken Steedman, have also been important to the timely production of this work. Both serve the successor to HAU, the Humber Archaeology Partnership (HAP).

A final word of thanks must go to the people of Beverley themselves, who have by their interest and support over the years encouraged, and ultimately made possible, the researches summarised in this book. We hope they like it.

Martin Foreman,
HAP, March 1998

A 16th-century gateway which was moved from the Friary precinct wall to the other side of Eastgate in the 1960s, where it remains today.

Nene Valley Railway

THE
TEDDY EXPRESS

Contents

Introduction 3
NVR beginnings 5
Peterborough Nene Valley 7
Peterborough to Orton Mere 8
Orton Mere 11
Orton Mere to Ferry Meadows 15
Ferry Meadows 16
Ferry Meadows to Wansford 18
Wansford 23
Wansford to Yarwell Junction 30
Yarwell Junction 32
Special events 34
Workshops 36
Filming 38
Locomotives 39
Mail by rail 43
Major projects 44
Volunteering 46
The 'Thomas' story 47
Shops and Cafe 48
Driving Experience Courses 48

Nene Valley Railway Milestones 13, 14, 17, 36, 39, 42, 43, 45

Title page: **YARWELL JUNCTION** USA Class 'S160' No 6046, owned by the Greg Wilson, is operating on loan to the NVR until 2015. Seen here on 5 July 2014 in capable charge of 'The Teddy Express', it arrives at Yarwell Junction, the current eastern terminus of the line. *Frances Townsend*

Introduction

The Nene Valley Railway is a 7½-mile standard gauge railway that operates between Yarwell Junction and Peterborough in Cambridgeshire. The main station and headquarters are to be found at Wansford, just off the main A1 trunk road and easily accessible from a large part of the country. The NVR is a steam railway, and can boast locomotives and rolling stock from as many as ten different countries.

The railway is very much a family attraction, being the home of *Thomas*, the children's favourite engine. It is also an educational charity that aims to bring back memories of railway travel of the past, particularly in the days of steam, for those who knew it, or to introduce those who are too young to have experienced it.

The Nene Valley Railway of today is the eastern section of the first railway to arrive in Peterborough, which ran from Blisworth via Northampton, Wellingborough, Thrapston, Oundle and Wansford. This was a branch from the London & Birmingham Railway's main line (opened in May 1838), and was known as the Blisworth, Northampton & Peterborough Railway, sanctioned by an Act of Parliament in 1843. In 1846 it was incorporated into the London & North Western Railway.

The very first passenger train along the Nene Valley arrived at Peterborough on Monday morning, 2 June 1845, and a crowd of more than 8,000 people welcomed the first train to arrive at the city, even though Peterborough's population was then less than 7,000. They filled the Fair Meadow and the station close to London Road. Church bells rang, bands played, and the railway passengers went off to

Above: **WANSFORD** station and signal box prior to closure. *NVR Archive*

enjoy inns, a waxworks exhibition, a theatre and the Market Place.

According to the *Stamford Mercury*, at 4 o'clock a second train from London arrived, causing 'extreme mortification, confusion and unpleasantness'. Passengers from the first train (who should have left an hour previously) filled the second, so when passengers from the second went to buy tickets home they found the train full. More carriages were found and filled. People packed the carriage roofs. Two men fought with sticks (then, because they were endangering women and children, adjourned the fight until the journey's end). Many were left behind.

When the train eventually left it was so overcrowded, with large numbers standing on the carriage roofs, that the guard had to stop it before the Lynch and Castor road overbridges to order people to 'duck' before the train could proceed! The *Stamford Mercury* said that 'it was gratifying everything had passed off so pleasantly'.

The railway was now in operation, but it had been a near thing. At a meeting in Thrapston, powerful land-owners had lined up against the intruder. The meeting had been attended by the Earl Fitzwilliam of Milton Estates, whose land was crossed by the line. The good Earl argued that the proposal was 'manifestly absurd', and he was supported by Lord Lilford and Lord Carysfoot of Elton. On the other hand, the Bishop of Peterborough gave considerable support to the enterprise, together with the Duke of Cleveland.

The new railway followed an 'easy' route along the lush water meadows of the River Nene, engineered by Robert Stephenson and George Bidder. It cost £429,409 (about £9,000 a mile), a remarkably low figure for that period, and took little more than a year to build.

Wansford Tunnel (617 yards) and the nearby bridges over the River Nene were major undertakings, and by the summer of 1844 some 1,000 men were working on them. Many of the men and some of their wives lived in earth huts, which were sometimes demolished by wind or quarrels. Labourers were paid 12 shillings a week, tunnel men 30 shillings. Accidents were frequent and a doctor was retained at £70 a year. The tunnel was cut from stone and soil, propped with wood, then lined with

bricks baked from Sibson and Yarwell clay.

Instances of rowdyism and fighting occurred frequently and as a result two police officers from Manchester were dispatched to Wansford to keep the peace. In Peterborough the local authorities, fearing the 'influx of bad characters', strengthened the city police force from four to five men!

The railway's first timetable showed five trains each day except Sundays, when there were two each way. The fastest Peterborough-Northampton train took 1¾ hours for the 42½ miles; London (Euston) was reached 3 hours later. The 3rd Class Peterborough-Northampton fare was 3s 7d, and the 3rd Class Peterborough-London fare 17 shillings. At first only a single track was laid, running on stone sleepers (examples of which are on display at Wansford), though bridges and tunnels were wide enough for two tracks. Trains left Peterborough and Blisworth at the same time and passed at Thrapston. Within months traffic was so heavy that by the end of 1846 a second track was in use; in that same year the line became part of the London & North Western Railway (LNWR).

This line was one of the first in the country to be equipped with electric telegraph apparatus, which was included from its inception. Despite the initial cost, this resulted in numerous operating advantages.

By now 'railway mania' had the country in its grip, with George Hudson, the 'Railway King', at its head. He aimed to extend the Midland Counties Railway (MCR) to Peterborough and on into the Fens via his Eastern Counties Railway (ECR), ahead of a rival line from London. The Syston & Peterborough Railway (Syston was a junction on the

MCR's Leicester to Derby line) was constructed in three sections, the Stamford to Peterborough section opening on 2 September 1846. Closely following this, the ECR from Ely via March arrived in Peterborough 10 months ahead of the contract date, opening to passengers on 14 January 1847. At this point Peterborough became a 'through' station, and it was now possible to reach London by two different lines. The missing link between the MCR and ECR was completed on 1 May 1848.

However, a direct line from London was now approaching the city. This was the Great Northern Railway (GNR) from Doncaster via Lincoln and Boston to Werrington Junction, which opened on 17 October 1848. The GNR line from the south opened on 5 October, 1850. Two years later, on 5 July 1852, the line was extended via Helpston, Tallington and Grantham to Retford (the 'Towns Line').

Peterborough's second link with East Anglia and the last major line to arrive, and was what became the Midland & Great Northern Joint Railway, which opened on 1 August 1866.

Three further openings had a direct influence on the Nene Valley line. In 1867 Wansford became a junction with the opening of the Sibson Extension (Wansford branch) of the Stamford & Essendine Railway. This single line joined the LNWR route 80 yards east of Wansford station and survived until 1 June 1929.

Before the 1870s, cross-country travel from Peterborough towards Birmingham was a tortuous journey along the Northampton line, then requiring a change of direction at Blisworth; this made the LNWR route considerably longer than the

Left: **WANSFORD** station as it was at closure of the line. After the takeover by the PRS the main platform was lengthened and a second platform was built on the wasteland in the foreground. *NVR Archive*

Right: **WANSFORD** station staff in 1910. Standing: Bertie Tilley (Station Master), Fred Middleton (Clerk), Fred Waite and Gerald Longfoot (Porters), F. C. Lee (Signal and Lineman). Seated: William Coles and Charles Kidsley (Signalmen). *NVR Archive*

competing Midland route via Leicester. On 1 November 1879 the LNWR opened an 11-mile connecting line from Yarwell Junction (west of Wansford) to Seaton on the LNWR's Rugby & Stamford Railway. The Peterborough-Rugby line was then developed as a secondary main line, linking Yarmouth with Birmingham, and Peterborough with North Wales and Ireland.

The third connecting line was the 1¾-mile Fletton Loop, which opened in 1883. This connected the Great Northern main line at Fletton Junction with the Nene Valley line at Longueville Junction, enabling GNR trains to run from Peterborough North to Leicester (Belgrave Road) via Rockingham, Medbourne and Lowesby Junction, and also provided access to Market Harborough and Melton Mowbray. Passenger services on the Loop (sometimes hauled by Patrick Stirling's famous 2-2-2 locomotives, which had a single central pair of 8-foot-diameter driving wheels) ended in 1916. Longueville Junction was removed in 1929, reinstated in 1947, taken out again in about 1961, and finally reinstated in 1974 to give the new Nene Valley Railway a connection to British Rail. Sugar beet traffic continued along the line until February 1991.

CASTOR station and level crossing in its heyday. *NVR Archive*

The LNWR ran Peterborough-Rugby and Peterborough-Northampton trains along the valley until the 1923 'Grouping' of railway companies, when the line became part of the London Midland & Scottish Railway (LMS).

In 1948 the railways were nationalised, but changes were few at first. However, in the 1950s and 1960s came a period of rationalisation. Traffic and services declined as passengers took to car and coach, and goods were increasingly conveyed by lorry. Stations were closed – Orton in 1942 and Castor and Wansford in 1957. Locomotives became run-down and dirty. Passenger trains between Peterborough and Northampton ceased on 2 May 1964, and there was no freight service beyond Oundle from that date. Wansford's goods facilities were withdrawn on 13 July 1964.

On the Rugby line the passenger service ended on 6 June 1966, just one week after the introduction of an improved electrified service from London via Rugby to Crewe and the North.

The Nene Valley's main surviving traffic was ironstone from Nassington Quarries, west of Wansford, but this service ceased in 1971. The thrice weekly goods service to Oundle and the occasional Oundle School special ceased in 1972, and British Rail closed the line completely. Thus the 127-year story came to what seemed to be a final conclusion.

However, although one chapter in the line's history had now closed, another was about to begin…

NVR beginnings

In 1968, just after the end of steam on British Rail, Richard Paten, an engineer who later became a local clergyman, purchased BR Class 5 4-6-0 No 73050 for £3,000, its scrap value, with the intention of displaying it on a plinth outside the local Technical College. Although BR had officially banned steam from its network, the locomotive travelled under its own power from Patricroft, Manchester, to New England locomotive shed in Peterborough under cover of darkness. Its arrival on 11 September 1968 generated considerable local interest. Because the locomotive was found to be in good condition there was resistance to the idea that No 73050 should be 'stuffed and mounted' – rather that it should be restored to full working order.

With the closure of New England shed that same month, the engine moved to a temporary storage compound at Peterborough East station. A more permanent home at the rail-connected Westwood Sidings of Baker Perkins Ltd followed, where volunteers commenced restoration work. By February 1970 the local branch, with 50 members, was sufficiently strong to form its own association, the Peterborough Locomotive Society (PLS).

On 28 March 1969 the Peterborough branch of the East Anglia Locomotive Preservation Society was established by 16 members. The aim of the society had been to purchase and restore the BR 'Pacific' locomotive No 70000 *Britannia*.

WANSFORD No 73050 on the coal road in July 1980. *Phil Horton*

CASTOR Hunslet 0-6-0ST *Jacks Green* passes Castor heading for the NVR's first Open Day at Wansford on 4 April 1974 *Brian Sharpe*

PETERBOROUGH *Jacks Green* comes off the main line. *NVR Archive*

Because of their similar aims, the society was now able to welcome the Peterborough group into its midst.

The following year BR was to remove the rail connection at Westwood, and No 73050 was moved to a new home at the British Sugar Corporation's Peterborough factory sidings, where it was joined by Hunslet 0-6-0 saddle tank locomotive *Jacks Green*, which had arrived, also under its own steam, when the local Nassington ironstone quarry closed. The PLS held its first public Open Day during Easter 1970, and its first steam day, with *Jacks Green*, a year later.

In the meantime important events were taking place on a broader front. In 1970 the Government's plan to relocate the old Clapham Transport Museum to York prompted the PLS to join forces with Peterborough Development Corporation; the city was now a 'New Town', and the population would double in the next 15 years. The City Council and the County Council submitted a detailed proposal

to set up a National Transport Museum based around the old Peterborough East station, which it was suggested should be run in conjunction with a preserved steam railway along the Nene Valley line.

Although it is regretted that this imaginative proposal was rejected, it was clear that there was still local support for a steam railway along the Nene Valley. In January 1972, in line with its wider interests, the PLS changed its name to the Peterborough Railway Society (PRS) and in March held a well-attended public meeting at the Town Hall, at which the idea of the Nene Valley Railway was formally launched.

PRS officers cooperated with the Development Corporation and the City and County Councils in the production of a feasibility report, which was published in June 1972. It supported the establishment of a steam railway through the heart of the future 2,000-acre Nene Park, which was to be developed as the leisure centrepiece of the new Greater Peterborough. With the announcement that BR was to close the surviving portion of the Northampton line, the PRS organised a last train to Oundle on 4 November 1972, after which the line officially closed.

In March 1974 the Peterborough Development Corporation bought the Nene Valley line between Longueville Junction and Yarwell Junction and leased it to the PRS to operate the railway – a major milestone in the society's history.

PETERBOROUGH The sugar beet factory where the Peterborough Railway Society (later NVR) gathered its early collection of rolling stock. *NVR Archive*

Peterborough Nene Valley

We start our journey along the line from the platform at Peterborough Nene Valley. The high-level girder bridge visible from the platform carries the East Coast Main Line, linking London King's Cross with the North and Scotland, and crosses the lower-level line that connects Peterborough's main-line station with March, Ely, Cambridge and other parts of East Anglia. The Nene Valley line used to continue beyond the buffer stops to join with this route at Peterborough East station, now sadly no more, just beyond the bridge.

Various locomotives and rolling stock are stored in the yard at Peterborough Nene Valley, including some belonging to Railworld, an independent environmental and transport project that has vehicles from around the world. The entire area between the station and the river was once the site of the LNWR's Woodston locomotive shed, which closed in 1932. In the 1950s the LNWR built coke ovens in this area to supply its early locomotives with fuel.

As the train draws out of Peterborough Nene Valley station, opened in 1986, we pass a signal box on the left, which came from Welland Bridge in Spalding, Lincolnshire.

Above: **PETERBOROUGH NENE VALLEY** BR Standard 5MT 4-6-0 No 73050 *City of Peterborough* runs round its train at Peterborough Nene Valley as a Central Trains unit passes on the line to March on 28 December 2005. *Brian Sharpe*

Left: **PETERBOROUGH NENE VALLEY** Hunslet Austerity 0-6-0ST No 22, formerly of the United Steel Companies, departs from the station. *Brian Sharpe*

Right: **PETERBOROUGH NENE VALLEY** Polish 'Kriegslok' 2-10-0 No 7173 leaves with a train on 30 March 1991. *Brian Sharpe*

Peterborough to Orton Mere

Our journey continues alongside the river, and soon we pass Woodston Staunch, once the site of the Co-op Wagon Works, which closed in 1963. On the left our train passes the site of the British Sugar Corporation's Peterborough factory (see also page 6), which closed in 1991 and is now redeveloped for residential use. One of the estate's roads is named 'Sugar Way' in recognition of the area's history. On the north side between the line and the river the old settling ponds have now been incorporated into the Woodston Ponds Nature Reserve, which opened in 2004 and is within walking distance of both Orton Mere

and Peterborough Nene Valley stations via the Nene Way footpath.

On the approach to Orton Mere the main-line link from Fletton Junction comes in from the left to join the NVR at Longueville Junction. Part of the Fletton Loop was used by BR right up until 1991; as a result, unlike other preserved railways with a BR connection, the NVR was unable to receive charter trains during the early years of preservation. In 1977 the section operated by BR had been upgraded effectively to passenger standards, in preparation for modern high-capacity wagons to be used for the seasonal sugar beet traffic.

Above left: **PETERBOROUGH NENE VALLEY** Class 56 diesel No 56057 arrives at Peterborough Nene Valley on 16 September 2005. *Brian Sharpe*

Left: **PETERBOROUGH NENE VALLEY** With the East Coast Main Line in the background, LNER 'A4' 'Pacific' No 60007 *Sir Nigel Gresley* heads a train of box vans on 17 June 1995. *Brian Sharpe*

Right: **PETERBOROUGH NENE VALLEY** LMS 'Black Five' 4-6-0 No 5231 accelerates away from Peterborough on 3 May 1992. *Brian Sharpe*

Above: **PETERBOROUGH NENE VALLEY** LNER 'V2' 2-6-2 No 4771 *Green Arrow* and 'B1' 4-6-0 No 1306 *Mayflower* double-head a train towards Longueville Junction on 9 September 2007. *Brian Sharpe*

Top right: **LONGUEVILLE JUNCTION** LMS 4F 0-6-0 No 44422 passes the junction on 23 February 2013 with the NVR's first steam passenger train along the Fletton Loop. *Brian Sharpe*

Right: **LONGUEVILLE JUNCTION** BR Standard 'Pacific' No 70000 *Britannia* visited the NVR for the February 2013 gala and is seen passing Longueville Junction with air-braked continental stock on the 24th of that month. *Brian Sharpe*

The section between the BSC sidings and Longueville Junction had been relaid by Society members in 1974, and this too now required upgrading to passenger standards.

Following the signing of a Private Siding Agreement with BR, a railway-chartered BR shuttle service first ran at 'Eurosteam 1980'. This was a success, with enthusiasts travelling long distances for the opportunity to ride over a line that had not seen regular passenger services since 1916!

In 1981 BR ran a properly advertised service on Sundays during the high season, then from 1982 to 1986 this changed to Saturday, which offered better main-line connections. With the opening of the Peterborough Extension to the Nene Valley station, the service ceased in 1986, although the line can still be used by visiting charter trains and by NVR locomotives travelling to and from BR open days and, latterly, Network Rail events.

LONGUEVILLE JUNCTION LNER 'B1' 4-6-0 No 1306 *Mayflower* passes the junction on 12 September 2004. *Brian Sharpe*

Orton Mere

A single platform at Orton Mere station was built by the Nene Valley Railway and opened in 1977; a second platform was added in March 1994, paid for by a bequest from a late member. The station has good access from all parts of Peterborough, and the platforms are situated partially under the bridge carrying Nene Parkway. A footpath crosses the river at the locks known as Orton Staunch, and gives access to Thorpe Wood golf course, built over the site of a Roman fort covering 27 acres. As many as 2,500 soldiers were stationed here between 44 and 65 AD.

Right: **ORTON MERE** LNER 'V2' 2-6-2 No 4771 *Green Arrow* heads a goods train through the station on 9 September 2007. *Brian Sharpe*

Left: **ORTON MERE** Visiting from Bressingham in Norfolk, Norwegian 'Mogul' No 377 *King Haakon VII* passes Orton Mere with a 'Santa special' on 17 December 2007. *Brian Sharpe*

Right: **ORTON MERE** With the late evening sun glistening off the side tanks, Polish 0-8-0T No 5485 departs from Orton Mere. *Brian Sharpe*

ORTON MERE GWR 4-6-0 No 4936 *Kinlet Hall* departs from Orton Mere on 11 September 2011. *Brian Sharpe*

Orton Mere was the eastern terminus of the line when it opened in 1977 but, being 2 miles by road from the city centre, visitors wishing to travel on the line understandably had difficulty locating it.

Back in 1974 a redundant ex-Midland Railway signal box had been obtained from Maxey Road crossing, Helpston, and was brought by road to the future Orton Mere station site. In 1976 the foundations for the box were constructed, although in the short term a ground frame was in operation. In 1978 a 12-lever frame from Nene Junction signal box was installed, complete with signals and associated interlocking. The box was designed so that it could be locked out of use when no signalman was on duty, but still permit trains to enter Orton Mere from Wansford.

Nene Valley Railway Milestones (1)

44-65AD		As many as 2,500 soldiers stationed at Orton Staunch Roman fort
1716		Milton Ferry bridge built
1791		Castor Water Mill built
1838	May	London-Blisworth-Birmingham main line opens
1845	June	First trains on Nene Valley line
1846	September	Stamford to Peterborough line opens
1847	14 January	Ely-March-Peterborough line opens
1848	1 May	Midland Counties Railway line completed
1848	17 October	Doncaster-Lincoln-Boston-Werrington Junction line opens
1850	5 October	GNR line from King's Cross opens
1852	5 July	Peterborough-Helpston-Tallington and Grantham-Retford line opens
1866	1 August	M&GN Joint line opens
1867		Wansford branch of Stamford & Essendine Railway opens
1879	1 November	Yarwell Junction to Seaton Junction (on Rugby-Stamford line) opens

Above: **ORTON MERE** The 12-lever signal box at Orton Mere is resplendent in its Midland Railway livery, having been rescued from Maxey Road crossing and restored by volunteers – a job very well done!

Left: **ORTON MERE** BR Standard 5MT 4-6-0 No 73050 *City of Peterborough* (left) meets LMS 'Black Five' 4-6-0 No 44837 at the station on 22 February 2014. *Brian Sharpe*

Left: **ORTON MERE** LMS 'Black Five' 4-6-0 No 45337, running as No 44837 (which worked the Peterborough-Northampton line on the last day of services in 1964), departs from Orton Mere on 22 February 2014. *Brian Sharpe*

Below left and below: **ORTON MERE** Approaching from Peterborough Nene Valley in March 1998, Class 'J27' 0-6-0 No 65894 hauls a rake of 'blood and custard' Mark 1 coaches into Orton Mere loop. The second view, looking towards Ferry Meadows, reveals that Platform 2 is yet to be built. No 65894 spent its final years in BR service working coal trains around its home shed of Sunderland (52G). Transferred on withdrawal to Tyne Dock for disposal, the loco was spared thanks to the efforts of the North Eastern Locomotive Preservation Group (NELPG), which stepped in to purchase it on 1 December 1976. *Both Phil Horton*

Nene Valley Railway Milestones (2)

Year	Date	Event
1883		Fletton Loop line opens
1916		Fletton Loop passenger traffic ends
1923		Railway 'Grouping' – Nene Valley line absorbed into LMS
1929		Longueville Junction removed
1929	1 June	Wansford branch of Stamford & Essendine Railway closes
1942		Orton station closes
1947		Longueville Junction reinstated
1948		Railways nationalised
1955		Rev Richard Paten visits North America and sees redundant locomotives on plinths
1957		Castor station closes
1957		Wansford station closes
1961 (circa)		Longueville Junction removed again
1964	13 July	Goods facilities at Wansford withdrawn
1964	2 May	Last passenger train from Peterborough to Northampton, and Oundle-Northampton line closes to goods traffic
1966	6 June	Peterborough-Rugby passenger service withdrawn
1968		Rev Richard Paten buys BR Class 5 4-6-0 No 73050 for £3,000
1969	28 March	Peterborough branch of the East Anglian Locomotive Preservation Society established
1970		Peterborough Locomotive Society formed

Above: **ORTON MERE** Admiring glances for ex-GWR 0-6-0PT No 6412 as it awaits departure with a goods train bound for Peterborough Nene Valley during the summer of 2007. *Both Phil Horton*

Orton Mere to Ferry Meadows

On leaving Orton Mere station the line runs along an embankment between flood plain meadows. We pass on our left Orton Water, and on the right the headquarters of the Peterborough Cruising Club. Shortly after the level crossing for the road serving the Yacht Club the line curves gently before entering a stretch of straight track leading to Ferry Meadows station.

Right: **ORTON MERE** PKP Ty2 No 7173, having just departed from Orton Mere in March 1991, has a clear road beyond the outer home signal visible in the middle distance. Ferry Meadows will be the next stop for this much-travelled locomotive, having seen service in Germany and Poland before arriving at the NVR. It was sold to Patrimoine Ferroviaire et Tourisme, a museum dedicated to the preservation of Belgian railway heritage. *Phil Horton*

Ferry Meadows

Until 1942 passengers arriving at this location would have been alighting at Overton station, latterly Orton Waterville. Despite the original station having closed to passengers in the midst of the Second World War, Orton Waterville was still open for goods traffic for a further 22 years until 18 December 1964. The only building from the original station remaining is what is believed to have been the coal office, located in the station yard opposite the new station building.

The present station building originally served as the Fletton Goods Office at Fletton, Peterborough, but in 1999 was dismantled and transported brick-by-brick to Ferry Meadows and rebuilt.

Below: **FERRY MEADOWS** The running-in board that greets visitors on arrival.

Right above and below (3): **FERRY MEADOWS** Clear directions for pedestrians and motorists!

Above: **FERRY MEADOWS** The old Fletton Goods Office, transformed into the station building, provides a perfect period feel at this 'new' station. The ticket office here also has a shop selling souvenirs, confectionery, ice creams, etc.

Below: **FERRY MEADOWS** The IRPS is based in the yard and runs the Overton Miniature Railway on selected days. *All Peter Townsend*

This is an excellent point for passengers to break their journey on the Nene Valley Railway and explore the park. Within a few hundred yards of the station are the park offices, information centre, snack bar and toilets. There is a large caravan and camping area, play areas for children, and a miniature steam railway, which runs from the information centre to Overton Lake sailing club.

The International Railway Preservation Society (IRPS) is restoring Wagons-Lits Restaurant Car No 2975 and Sleeping Car No 3916, which are owned by the NVR. To help preserve these vehicles the IRPS is working with the NVR and the railway's Travelling Post Office Group to build a state-of-the-art facility at Ferry Meadows station. Plans for 'The Night Mail Museum' include a museum building, running shed and restoration facilities on site for all their work. It will house an ever-expanding postal archive and the archive of Wagons-Lits material, with the late George Behrend's collection at its heart, from its origins to the present day.

Nene Valley Railway Milestones (3)

1970		National Transport Museum based at old Peterborough East station proposal rejected
1970	Easter	PLS holds first Public Open Day
1971		Nassington quarry ironstone trains withdrawn
1971		Rev W. Awdry names Hudswell Clarke No 1800 *Thomas*
1971	Easter	PLS holds first steam day featuring 0-6-0ST *Jacks Green*
1972	January	PLS changes name to Peterborough Railway Society (PRS)
1972		Thrice-weekly Oundle goods service withdrawn

Right and above right: **FERRY MEADOWS** 'You are here', as the expression goes! There's a useful map on the side wall of the station building, while the train departures board provides information on train services on running days.

Far right: **FERRY MEADOWS** Running tender-first, USA 'S160' Class No 6046 awaits departure for Orton Mere and Peterborough Nene Valley on 5 July 2014. One wonders if the neat and trim appearance of the station is the talking point between members of the train staff, or could it have been the Tour de France taking place in Yorkshire over that weekend? We will never know! *All Peter Townsend*

Ferry Meadows to Wansford

Ferry Meadows Country Park, the centrepiece of the Nene Park Trust, has three lakes; covering 120 acres, they were the result of gravel excavation. The largest of them, Overton Lake, can be seen to the north of the railway, with Milton Ferry bridge, built in 1716, in the distance.

Above: **FERRY MEADOWS** These three views taken at Ferry Meadows show the approach to Ham Lane level crossing, where the line crosses the access road to Ferry Meadows Country Park, followed by a look back towards the station with a train departing, and a look ahead towards Wansford on 4 July 2014. *Peter Townsend*

Left: **LYNCH BRIDGE** An aerial view of Hunslet 0-6-0ST No 75006 crossing the bridge. *NVR Archive*

Above right: **MILL LANE BRIDGE** French Nord Compound 4-6-0 No 23.268 has just passed under Mill Lane bridge, Castor, on 20 September 1986. *Brian Sharpe*

As we leave Ferry Meadows station we go over Ham Lane crossing, complete with flashing red lights that warn drivers to stop to allow the passage of trains. Continuing our journey we enter a wooded cutting and the line rises as we approach Alwalton Lynch. The line crosses the River Nene for the first time at Lynch Bridge, where a speed restriction applies due to the restricted clearances for continental rolling stock.

The line rises on a gradient of 1 in 270 as we approach and pass under Mill Lane bridge. This carries a road that leads from the villages of Castor and Ailsworth to the old Castor Mill. It is interesting to note that the bridge was partially constructed from old stone blocks once used instead of timber sleepers when the London & Birmingham Railway was being built in 1837. These blocks were also used to construct the facade of Wansford Tunnel.

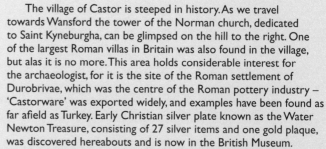

The village of Castor is steeped in history. As we travel towards Wansford the tower of the Norman church, dedicated to Saint Kyneburgha, can be glimpsed on the hill to the right. One of the largest Roman villas in Britain was also found in the village, but alas it is no more. This area holds considerable interest for the archaeologist, for it is the site of the Roman settlement of Durobrivae, which was the centre of the Roman pottery industry – 'Castorware' was exported widely, and examples have been found as far afield as Turkey. Early Christian silver plate known as the Water Newton Treasure, consisting of 27 silver items and one gold plaque, was discovered hereabouts and is now in the British Museum.

Our train now passes over Ermine Street, the famous Roman road much of which became the original course of the A1 trunk road. There is, however, no visible sign of it crossing our path. This is also true of the location of the former Castor station, closed in 1957 and long since demolished.

Once over Castor crossing, Water Newton can be seen on

Above: **MILL LANE BRIDGE** The ex-Swedish Railways (SJ) railcar No Y7 1212 approaches the bridge on 16 August 1988. *Phil Horton*

Above left and left: **MILL LANE BRIDGE** Comparing the views looking back towards Ferry Meadows station (top) and towards Wansford (below) taken on 4 July 2014 with the pictures from 1986, 1988 and 1991 clearly illustrates the changing landscape, with considerably more tree and foliage growth. *Peter Townsend*

Right: **MILL LANE BRIDGE** In green livery, BR Standard 5MT 4-6-0 No 73050 *City of Peterborough* passes Castor on 23 March 1996. *Brian Sharpe*

Above: **CASTOR** LNER 'B1' 4-6-0 No 1306 *Mayflower* is immaculately turned out on 4 April 2003, which is not surprising as this was a private 'runpast' exclusively for *Heritage Railway* magazine's Deputy Editor Brian Sharpe during the locomotive's first run down the line with a train after completion of its restoration. No 1306 was rostered for its first public passenger run the following day. *Brian Sharpe*

Below: **WANSFORD** Ex-GWR 'Hall' Class 4-6-0 No 4920 crosses the girder viaduct on the approach to the river crossing at Wansford in the summer of 1999. The erstwhile Stamford branch left the main line at a point roughly behind the second carriage. *Phil Horton*

Above: **CASTOR** Ex-Swedish Railways No 1928 rattles along the 3-mile straight on its way to Peterborough in May 1998. Note Castor's church spire in the distance. *Phil Horton*

our left. Also on our left we pass the Sutton Cross Travelling Post Office (TPO) lineside apparatus, the first of two sets to be installed by the NVR, of which more later. The line now begins to curve to the left and runs on an embankment some 400 yards long, carrying it above the flood plain of the River Nene.

Just before we cross the river on a lattice girder bridge there is a short viaduct that allows flood waters easy passage beneath the trackbed. Just short of the bridge was the junction with the line from Stamford, which closed in 1929; all that remains of its course are the overgrown embankments curving away to our right towards the village of Sutton. However, a recent survey surprisingly found that some buildings were still standing at all the intermediate stations, more than 65 years after closure!

Be sure to look out of the carriage windows as we cross the river, as there are often ducks and perhaps a swan or two gliding downstream. This is also a favourite spot for permit-holding anglers.

On the right immediately after crossing the river can be seen a real gem in terms of railway preservation – the 60-lever Wansford signal box. Built in 1907, this box replaced no fewer than three earlier boxes. The level crossing over which we now pass is controlled by the signalman, and the road was once the main A1 trunk road – thank goodness for the dual carriageway that now carries the traffic past Wansford! Our train now slows for arrival at Wansford station.

Right: **WANSFORD** Norwegian 'Mogul' No 377 *King Haakon VII* crosses the River Nene and arrives at Wansford on 17 December 2007. *Brian Sharpe*

Right and far right: **WANSFORD** During March 1998 departing 'J27' Class 0-6-0 No 65894 runs tender-first outwards from Wansford past the signal box, then returns smokebox-first, having run round its train at Orton Mere. *Both Phil Horton*

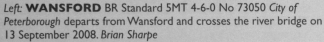

Left: **WANSFORD** BR Standard 5MT 4-6-0 No 73050 *City of Peterborough* departs from Wansford and crosses the river bridge on 13 September 2008. *Brian Sharpe*

Below left: **WANSFORD** LMS 4F 0-6-0 No 44422 is captured glistening in the evening sun on 17 January 2010 as it leaves the station. The River Nene is in spate after some very heavy rain during the preceding few days. *Brian Sharpe*

Bottom: **WANSFORD** Preservation takes many forms! The 60-lever 1907-built Wansford signal box contrasts here with a 1976-built MGB Roadster, both still going strong in July 2014. *Frances Townsend*

Right: Also restored to life is this fine example of one of the many, although perhaps less obvious, examples of station furniture that go to help make the realism, atmosphere and all-round visitor experience that bit more memorable. *Frances Townsend*

Wansford

Wansford is the headquarters and main operating base of the Nene Valley Railway. There is much to see and do at this station, so be sure to allow plenty of time to explore.

Right: **WANSFORD** Newly restored Southern Railway Bulleid 'Battle of Britain' Class 'Pacific' No 34081 *92 Squadron* arrives at Wansford on 20 July 1998. *Brian Sharpe*

Far right: **WANSFORD** A closer view of the impressive signal gantry at the Peterborough end of the station. The larger arms are the Wansford starter signals, while the smaller 'dolly' arms are for 'calling on'. *Frances Townsend*

Above: **WANSFORD** The impressive entrance to the station. *Frances Townsend*

Right: **WANSFORD** LNER 'A3' 'Pacific' No 60103 *Flying Scotsman* departs from Wansford with a train of box vans on 8 July 1994. *Brian Sharpe*

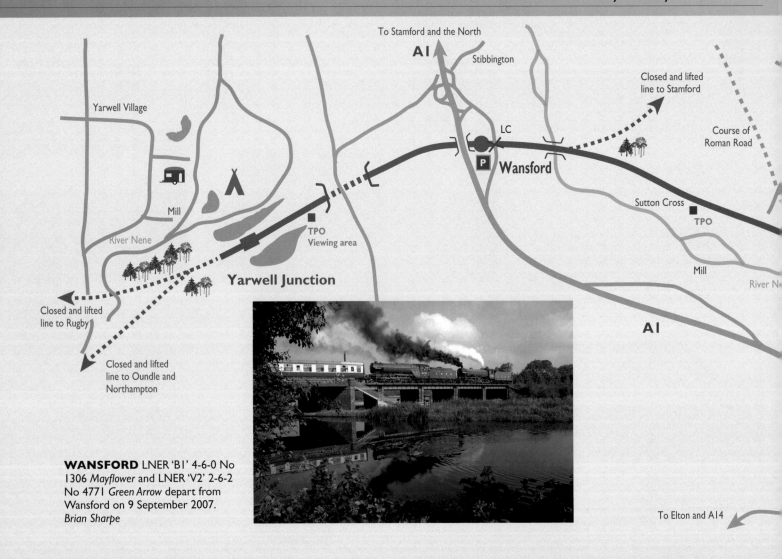

To Stamford and the North

A1

Stibbington

Yarwell Village

Closed and lifted
line to Stamford

LC

Course of
Roman Road

P   Wansford

Mill

Sutton Cross

River Nene

TPO
Viewing area

TPO

Yarwell Junction

Mill

River Ne

Closed and lifted
line to Rugby

A1

Closed and lifted
line to Oundle and
Northampton

WANSFORD LNER 'B1' 4-6-0 No
1306 *Mayflower* and LNER 'V2' 2-6-2
No 4771 *Green Arrow* depart from
Wansford on 9 September 2007.
Brian Sharpe

To Elton and A14

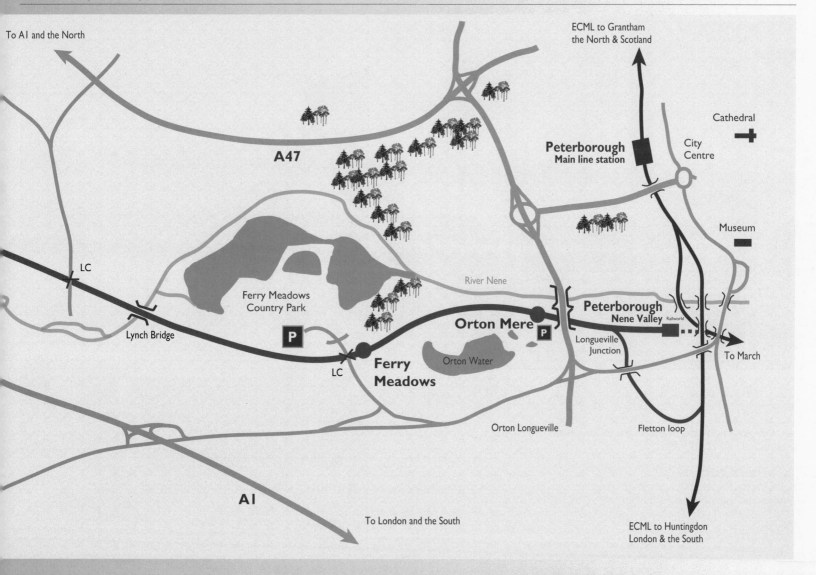

To A1 and the North

ECML to Grantham
the North & Scotland

A47

Cathedral

Peterborough
Main line station

City
Centre

Museum

LC

River Nene

Ferry Meadows
Country Park

P

Peterborough
Nene Valley

Railworld

Orton Mere

P

Lynch Bridge

LC

Ferry
Meadows

Orton Water

Longueville
Junction

To March

Orton Longueville

Fletton loop

A1

To London and the South

ECML to Huntingdon
London & the South

Above: **WANSFORD** US Army Transportation Corps 'S160' 2-8-0 No 5197 departs from Wansford on 8 June 2007, between Class 47 No 47270 and Class 31 No 31271.

Top right: **WANSFORD** Visiting NER 'J27' 0-6-0 No 65894 departs from the station westbound on 19 April 1998.

Right: **WANSFORD** Swedish 2-6-4T No 1928 arrives during the railway's opening weekend on 7 June 1977. Note the difference in signalling – in the early years two single-post signals were used, the one on the left carrying a rare example of an early GNR 'somersault' arm. The more recent views show the replacement gantry. *All Brian Sharpe*

WANSFORD The sight of three powerful locomotives is proving very popular with visitors of all ages during the 2011 gala weekend. On 11 September ex-GWR 4-6-0 No 4936 *Kinlet Hall* arrives at Wansford, passing BR Standard 5MT 4-6-0 No 73050 *City of Peterborough* and BR Standard 8P 'Pacific' No 71000 *Duke of Gloucester*. *Brian Sharpe*

Above: **WANSFORD** Ex-Danish Railways No 656 *Tinkerbell*, Hudswell Clarke 0-6-0T *Thomas* and Hunslet 0-6-0ST *Jacks Green* take part in one of the railway's popular Industrial Weekend events during the early years. *NVR Archive*

Above: **WANSFORD** In September 1978 the 67-foot Wansford locomotive turntable was commissioned. Originally of 60-foot diameter, it was built in 1933 by Ransomes & Rapier of Ipswich for Bourne station, but in 1960 was removed to Peterborough East station, from where it was moved again to Wansford. BR Standard 8P 'Pacific' No 71000 *Duke of Gloucester* amply illustrates the need for the extra 7 feet as it is carefully positioned on the turntable on 11 September 2011 during the gala weekend. *Brian Sharpe*

Right: **WANSFORD** Recreating scenes from the past is an important part of the atmosphere of a preserved railway, and a demonstration goods train provides an essential element. Here Barclay 'Austerity' 0-6-0ST No 15 of the Wemyss Private Railway arrives at Wansford with just such a goods train on 27 April 2008. *Brian Sharpe*

Above: **WANSFORD** Ex-Swedish Railways 'B' Class 4-6-0 No 101 and LNER 'B1' 4-6-0 No 1306 *Mayflower* pass at Wansford.

Top right: **WANSFORD** Southern Railway 'S15' 4-6-0 No 841 *Greene King* and ex-German Railways Class '64' 2-6-2T No 64.305 were photographed at Wansford on 28 March 1978.

Right: **WANSFORD** BR Standard 5MT 4-6-0 No 73050 *City of Peterborough*, in lined black livery but without her customary nameplates, crosses the level crossing on 11 September 2011. *All Brian Sharpe*

Time now to rejoin our train for the onward journey to Yarwell Junction, which takes us under the A1 trunk road and into Wansford Tunnel.

Wansford to Yarwell Junction

Wansford is a through station and the main base of the NVR, and its easy access from the A1 trunk road makes it the preferred joining point for many people.

Trains starting here usually depart to the west towards Yarwell Junction. Once under way, the train passes under the A1, then runs through a steep cutting before entering Wansford Tunnel, which is 617 yards in length. The tunnel is straight and level and has no ventilation shafts.

As we leave the darkness the line curves gently south in a wooded cutting. Keep an eye out on the right shortly after leaving the tunnel as we pass a platelayers' hut that has been named Hallett's Halt, in recognition of the efforts of a volunteer who helped secure a Heritage Lottery Grant for the TPO Group

Top left: **WANSFORD TUNNEL** USA 'S160' Class No 6046, seen here on 5 July 2014, emerges from the darkness of the tunnel with 'The Teddy Express' on its way to Yarwell Junction. *Peter Townsend*

Bottom left: **WANSFORD TUNNEL** One of 149 de Glehn-du Bosquet Class 3.513 4-6-0 locomotives built for French Railways, No 3.628 (SNCF No 230 D 116) ran for a number of years on the NVR and is seen leaving the tunnel. This loco subsequently returned to France and now resides in Longueville roundhouse. *NVR Archive*

Below: **HALLETT'S HALT** On 7 April 2006 BR Standard 5MT 4-6-0 No 73050 *City of Peterborough* passes the platelayers' hut that became Hallett's Halt, heading the first passenger train since the run-round loop was relaid. *Brian Sharpe*

to install a second set of apparatus, which we pass on the left shortly thereafter. Between trains this is a very tranquil and peaceful spot on the line; as with other locations, there is a visitor information board at the TPO viewing area.

Passing the ground frame that operates the points for the siding and run-round loop, the train now slows for arrival at Yarwell Junction station.

Left: **Near HALLETT'S HALT** The TPO lineside apparatus viewing area can be reached by the lineside footpath from Yarwell Junction.

Below left and below: **HALLETT'S HALT** No passenger trains call here and, as the sign clearly points out, there is definitely 'No public access' to the 'Halt'.

Below right (2): **YARWELL JUNCTION** Just short of the platform at Yarwell Junction is the ground frame that operates the points for the run-round loop.

Above: **HANNAH'S BRIDGE** Just short of the station eagle-eyed passengers might spot a sign on a bridge spanning a stream. It is named Hannah's bridge in recognition of the huge fund-raising and supporting work undertaken by Hannah and Bill Forman; without them, many volunteers and the Army, Yarwell Junction station and memorial garden would not have been built so early in the railway's preservation days. *All Peter Townsend*

Yarwell Junction

Yarwell Junction station is situated on an embankment south of the River Nene and between the Sibson Fisheries. The track layout here was altered around Easter 2006 to provide additional siding space, and the platform was opened at Easter 2007. An LNWR-style period station building has been constructed on the platform.

By the use of country footpaths it is possible to break your journey and explore the old-world villages of Yarwell and Nassington. Look out for the Country Walk leaflets available from time to time at the railway's booking offices. Please note that some of the paths are rather rough and not suitable for those who have difficulty in walking, and parts are also subject to flooding. A river-boat link to and from Wansford is planned.

Bottom far left: **YARWELL JUNCTION** The approach to the station on 4 July 2014.

Left: **YARWELL JUNCTION** The LNWR-style station building is a credit to the hard work and enthusiasm of the NVR volunteers, not just in its original construction but also in its upkeep. There is a memorial garden here where friends and family of supporters and volunteers who have taken their 'final journey' can spend a little time in remembrance.

Left: **YARWELL JUNCTION** A place to take the weight off your feet perhaps!

Below left and below: **YARWELL JUNCTION** This is the end of the line looking towards the buffer stops, with the neat and tidy appearance of the station area providing a pleasant environment to await the next train. Timetable details can be found on the notice board beneath the traditional running-in board. *All Frances Townsend*

Above: **YARWELL JUNCTION** 'Running round' at Yarwell:
1. The loco uncouples and moves slowly forward. The fireman can just be seen at the point lever in preparation.
2. Having moved onto the 'headshunt', the points are changed and the loco slowly reverses along the far line…
3. …passing behind the carriages to the other end of the loop.
4. The fireman steps carefully down from the loco and, once it has cleared the points, uses the lever frame seen on page 31 to set the road for the loco to move forward into the platform road.
5. The loco is recoupled ready for the return journey to Wansford and beyond. *All Frances Townsend*

Right: **YARWELL JUNCTION** LMS 4F 0-6-0 No 44422 stands at the station at the western end of the NVR on a wonderfully bright and crisp winter's day, 17 January 2010. *Brian Sharpe*

There is a footpath to the viewing area just west of the tunnel to enable visitors to see the spectacle of trains emerging from it. The Travelling Post Office mail exchange apparatus is also to be found near the tunnel mouth.

Once the locomotive has changed ends ('run round'), the train heads eastwards, retracing its tracks back through the tunnel to Wansford.

Special events

Throughout the year a wide variety of special events are held at the NVR. Although the dates and exactly what is happening can change from year to year, there is an emphasis on variety and the programme is refreshed on a regular basis, making a return visit worthwhile.

The NVR's recent events have included:

Murder Mystery Evenings
Summer Strawberry Specials
Classic Weekend (Classic Road Vehicles)
Class 14s at 50
'A Weekend on the Continent'
Le Train Bleu Foncé
Mixed Traffic Steam Gala Weekend
Tornado Grand Rail Mail Event
Tornado TPO photo shoot
Steam and diesel enthusiasts' galas
'The Jolly Fisherman' (fish & chip supper)

Real Ale Festival
Vintage vehicle events (large displays of steam traction engines and vintage and classic vehicles)
1960s Weekend

In addition to all of these, Santa visits the railway every December.
     Such is the popularity of events, advance booking where possible is recommended as places are limited on some special trains.

Right: **WANSFORD** HRH Prince Edward visited the NVR on 1 June 2007 during the railway's 30th anniversary celebrations, and drove LNER 'B1' 4-6-0 No 61306 *Mayflower*.

Left: **WANSFORD** On the 150th anniversary of the opening of the Northampton & Peterborough Railway, replica Stockton & Darlington Railway 0-4-0 *Locomotion* worked a train along the NVR on 27 September 1975. *Brian Sharpe*

Below: **WANSFORD** BR Standard 5MT 4-6-0 No 73050 *City of Peterborough* departs from Wansford on 28 December 2005 with a post-Christmas service.

Above: **WANSFORD** Hudswell Clarke 0-6-0T *Thomas* stands at Wansford in seasonal conditions on 28 December 2005. At the time of writing *Thomas* is in the locomotive 'hospital' and is unable to see his fans or pull trains until 2015. However, it may still be possible to arrange a 'Thomas'-themed party pulled by one of *Thomas*'s bigger friends. *Brian Sharpe*

Above right: **YARWELL** *Thomas* emerges from the Yarwell end of Wansford Tunnel. *Brian Sharpe*

Left: **FERRY MEADOWS** This little chap was spotted aboard 'The Teddy Bear' express on 5 July 2014. *Peter Townsend*

Right: **CASTOR** BR Standard 'Pacific' No 70000 *Britannia* accelerates away from the river bridge at Castor with a 'Santa special' on 19 December 1981. *Brian Sharpe*

Nene Valley Railway Milestones (4)

Year	Date	Event
1972		Oundle School special trains cease to run
1972		British Rail closes line completely after 127 years' service
1972	4 November	PRS special last train to Oundle
1972	June	PRS, Peterborough Development Corporation, City and County Councils prepare NVR feasibility report
1972	March	PRS holds public meeting to launch idea of Nene Valley Railway
1973		British Rail gives PRS permission to use Wansford signal box as its new Wansford base
1973	March	Ex-Swedish Railways 2-6-4T Class 'S1' No 1928 arrives at BSC sidings
1973	September	First stock arrives and first works train runs
1973	3 November	Tenancy agreement signed with British Rail for Wansford site
1974		Longueville Junction reinstated by NVR to open link with main line
1974		Berne loading gauge adopted
1974		Stock moved to Wansford from BSC sidings
1974		Ex-Midland Railway signal box from Maxey Road, Helpston, acquired
1974	Easter	Wansford Steam Centre opens to the public for the first time
1974	March	Peterborough Development Corporation buys Nene Valley line between Longueville and Yarwell Junctions

Workshops

In 1980 the first stage of the locomotive shed had been erected with associated working facilities. Steelwork for the 60-foot-long two-road building had been obtained from the old Peterborough Pig Market. Phase two doubled the length of the shed, and in 1983 film revenue from the James Bond film *Octopussy* paid for a single-road carriage and wagon shed, new access being provided from a point west of the A1 road bridge.

Below: **WANSFORD** The extensive workshops are viewed from the patio area of the Turntable Cafe on 5 July 2014. *Peter Townsend*

Above: **WANSFORD** 2004 saw the arrival of ex-BR diesel-powered Plasser GB 45-ton TASC track maintenance machine No DR 98500. It was built in 1985 for track inspection and minor works, primarily for use on rural branch lines in Scotland, and in February 2005 was obtained in vandalised condition from Amey Rail at Perth Depot. *Peter Townsend*

Following the opening of the Peterborough Extension in 1986, it was time again to turn to less glamorous but no less vital tasks. A four-road locomotive storage shed was added south of the existing shed, the steelwork having been obtained from redundant London Brick Company drying sheds. At last the majority of the NVR locomotive fleet could for the moment be kept under cover.

During September 1993 the Wansford loco yard was relaid, enabling easier loading and unloading of locomotives from road transport. The new yard also gave extra siding space and more manoeuvrability for the locomotives, as well as an opportunity for additional platform space adjacent to the new Wansford station building.

Early in 2006 the site for a further extension to the Wansford locomotive shed was cleared. The

new shed, the Heavy Overhaul Workshop, partly financed by an NVR member, took around two years to complete. It is 134 feet long and 60 feet wide, with one track, and includes a much-needed new machine shop, overhead crane, mess room and toilets. By Easter 2007 all the steelwork and most of the external cladding were up, with £125,000 having been spent on the project; all was completed by the end of that year.

Below left and below: **WANSFORD** The viewing gallery at the workshops at Wansford is well worth visiting, and is just a short walk from the main station building. Always a hive of activity, there are locomotives in various stages of overhaul. On 5 July 2014 the frames of 'Battle of Britain' Class 4-6-2 No 34081 *92 Squadron* can be seen in the company of its distinctive blue and red wheel sets and various parts from Hudswell Clarke 0-6-0T *Thomas*. Both these locomotives are undergoing major overhaul, and when complete they will receive new 10-year boiler certificates and a new lease of life. *Peter Townsend*

Above: **WANSFORD** Restoration of BR Class 14 No D9520 is nearing completion and the 'good as new' appearance of the inner workings is plain to see! This locomotive carries a 'Built 1964 Swindon' works plate and an 86A Newport (Ebbw Junction) shed plate, visible to the right of the steps. Affectionately named 'Teddy Bears' by enthusiasts, this is one of 56 examples built, of which amazingly some 20 have been spared the cutter's torch.

Above right and right: **WANSFORD** Restoration and preservation is painstaking work, be it fabricating new parts from sheet metal or rubbing down and varnishing woodwork. The workforce of volunteers derives reward and satisfaction from seeing the finished item – as indeed do visitors to the railway.

Filming

Between 1977 and the end of 2014 more than 170 films, including commercials and episodes for television, have been made on the Nene Valley Railway. Notable films include the Bond films *Octopussy and Goldeneye, The Dirty Dozen: Next Mission* and Television filming has included *Secret Army, Reilly Ace of Spies, Hannay* and *Poirot*. Commercial films have been set on or around the line, which often forms a distinctive backdrop, while current affairs programmes, pop videos and railway-orientated films have been made with impressive results.

The Nene Valley Railway lends itself naturally to filming by having a number of features that, when combined, provide a formidable bonanza of alternatives for film companies. The railway has 7½ miles of track running over and alongside a river, it traverses meadowland, cuttings and urban areas, passes an industrial complex, and runs through a country park. Features such as an imposing Victorian station building, a tunnel more than 600 yards long, and an old-fashioned manually operated four-gate level crossing controlled from a 60-lever signal box all provide diverse and historic settings that are carefully nurtured by all concerned. The availability of locomotives and rolling stock of both British and foreign origin provides a wide range of opportunities and subjects for film makers.

During the 1990s films shot on the NVR included another Bond film, *GoldenEye*, and a two-part episode of *London's Burning*. Since 2000 the NVR has continued to provide a location for a variety of films for the big screen and television as well as for commercials, videos, regular news items, etc. These range from major big-budget productions such as Spielberg's war epic *Band of Brothers* in 2000, which used the Belgian and Norwegian carriages (for the latter's US-style open verandas) as well as the Wagons-Lits dining car.

The BBC often uses NVR facilities for its historical dramas, documentaries and 'soaps'. In 2003 the mouth of Wansford Tunnel featured in an episode of BBC TV's *Casualty* about a train crash. In 2004 scenes around Castor crossing appeared in *Silent Witness* (a crash involving a Land Rover on the tracks). For a 2005 film featuring Agatha Christie's Hercule Poirot, *Murder on the Blue Train*, Wansford became a Paris station! Also in 2005 an episode of *Dalziel and Pascoe*, involving a football coach accident, was filmed at Wansford level crossing.

The railway has featured in regional documentaries such as Anglia TV's *Riddles of the River* (about the Nene) in 2001 and *Walking the Nene Way* in 2005. Filming in 2006/07 included material for Network Rail and the TV series *Country Lives*.

WANSFORD TUNNEL During the filming of the James Bond film *Octopussy* in 1983, Swedish 'B' Class 4-6-0 No 1697 has a confrontation with a Mercedes on the track near Wansford Tunnel. *Brian Sharpe*

Locomotives

The Nene Valley Railway is home to a wide variety of locomotives, and as has been seen these are of both British and European origin. In addition to the home-based fleet, visiting locomotives make regular appearances on the line for a variety of reasons. First and foremost is the hiring in of locomotives from other preserved lines and organisations for special events. However, an increasingly important development at the NVR since the reopening of the main-line connection via the Fletton Loop has been the servicing, maintenance and stabling of steam locomotives ticketed for main-line running.

The NVR has always had a strong diesel presence, and this continues with both the home fleet and visiting locomotives.

WANSFORD Nos 31271, 57057 and Class 40 D306 *Atlantic Conveyor* line up at Wansford on 16 September 2005. *Brian Sharpe*

Nene Valley Railway Milestones (5)

1974	March	PRS leases Nene Valley line between Longueville and Yarwell Junctions from PDC
1975		British Rail removes track east of Longueville Junction on Fletton Loop
1975	Easter	First steam shuttle service operates from Wansford through tunnel to Yarwell
1976	January	Lynch Bridge demolished. Continental locos and stock moved to Wansford from BSC sidings
1976		Danish 'F' Class 0-6-0T arrives
1976		French Nord express passenger locomotive arrives
1976		'Battle of Britain' Class No 34081 *92 Squadron* arrives from Barry scrapyard
1976	Summer	Orton Mere run-round loop installed and platform construction started
1976	September	67ft Wansford turntable (ex-Bourne and Peterborough East) commissioned
1977	1 January	First General Manager appointed
1977		Old wooden station building from Barnwell acquired, moved to Wansford and erected on Platform 2
1977	24 May	Major Rose, Railway Inspector, passes railway for passenger services
1977	1 June	Official opening of Wansford-Orton Mere section

Just as locomotives visit the NVR from other lines, so locomotives normally based on the NVR spend time away from home attending galas and special events.

As an example, the following table lists the locomotives based on the NVR as of July 2014, and is intended as a representation of the variety of motive power that visitors are likely to see.

Number	Name/builder	Class	Built
Operational			
73050	*City of Peterborough/* BR Derby Works	5MT	1954
D9520	BR Swindon Works	14	1964
9525	BR Swindon Works	14	1964
31108	Brush	31	1959
22	Hunslet	Industrial	1956
DL83	Sentinel	Industrial	1967
-	Barabel/Sentinel	Industrial	1964
50	*Stanton No 50/* Yorkshire Engine Co	Industrial	1958
1212	Eksjoverken	Swedish 'Y7' railcar	1958
Under overhaul			
34081	*92 Squadron/* Southern Railway, Brighton Works	'Battle of Britain'	1948
656	*Tinkerbell/*Frichs, Aarhus	Danish 'F'	1949
1800/1	*Thomas/*Hudswell Clarke	Industrial	1947
801	Alco	Industrial	1949
323 674 2	DRG	Industrial	1952

Number	Name/builder	Class	Built
2896	*Frank/*F. C. Hibberd & Co	Industrial	1944
1178	Motala	'S'	1914
2945	*Toby/*Cockerill	Industrial	1890
Stored			
5485	Fablok, Poland	'Slask' TKP	1959
63.305	Krupps, Germany	'64'	1936
1539	*Derek Crouch/* Hudswell Clarke	Industrial	1924
1953	*Jacks Green/*Hunslet	Industrial	1939

Below: **WANSFORD** Restoration is a long and complex process and, once dismantled, the parts can take up a considerable amount of space! Seen here stored in Wansford works yard on 5 July 2014 is the boiler of *92 Squadron*, awaiting restoration of the main frames. The flat wagon makes this very heavy item movable as and when required to facilitate other stock moves in the busy yard. *Peter Townsend*

Above: **WANSFORD** Ex-London Transport Sentinel No DL83 awaits its next task on 5 July 2014. *Peter Townsend*

Right: **CASTOR** A recent regular visitor to the line, new-build LNER Peppercorn 'A1' 'Pacific' No 60163 *Tornado* approaches Castor. The A1 Steam Locomotive Trust – a registered charity – built this completely new 'A1', all the original LNER variants having been scrapped. Built to the original design and with the help of the latest technology, No 60163 is fitted with additional water capacity and the latest railway safety electronics, and is therefore fully equipped for today's main-line railway.

Above: **WANSFORD** 'Teddy Bear' No D9520 is peeping out of the workshop wearing an appropriate reporting number '2014' as this shot was captured on 5 July of that year. Preparations were under way to ensure that this and sister loco No 9525 would both be ready for the special 'Class 14s at 50' event on Saturday 16 August 2014. *Peter Townsend*

Far left: **WANSFORD** Class 'A2' 4-6-2 No 60532 *Blue Peter* is seen at Wansford in the winter of 1996/97 in BR lined green livery. *Phil Horton*

Left: **WANSFORD** 'Entente cordial': a transformed Class 'A2' 4-6-2, now No 1457 *Blue Peter* and in LNER Apple Green, is seen at the water column in Wansford yard sharing a moment in the company of French Nord De Glehn Compound No 3.628. The latter loco has since returned to France, where it is hoped to restore her to main-line running condition. *NVR Archive*

Nene Valley Railway Milestones (6)

1977	4 June	First NVR public services on Wansford-Orton Mere section commence
1977	December	First 'Santa specials' run on the NVR
1978	17 May	Ferry Meadows station opens
1983	End	Outline planning permission granted for reinstatement of Fletton Loop
1984	2 May	Extension appeal launched to fund relaying of Fletton Loop
1985	February	HRH Prince Edward pays unofficial visit as part of Cambridge University Rag Week
1986	24 May	First passenger train arrives at Peterborough Nene Valley station
1986	30 June	HRH Prince Edward returns to officially open the extension from Orton Mere to Peterborough Nene Valley
1987	July	Ex-London Transport Barking water tank arrives, subsequently erected at Peterborough Nene Valley
1990		Four Belgian carriages arrive
1991	February	Fletton Loop sugar beet traffic ends
1993	September	Wansford loco yard tracks relaid
1994	March	Second platform opened at Orton Mere
1995	September	New £250,000 Wansford station building officially opens
1998		'Battle of Britain' Class No 34081 *92 Squadron* enters NVR service after 21-year restoration
1998		Class 117 DMU enters NVR service

Right: **WANSFORD** Cockerill tram engine No 2945 is seen in September 1996. Phil Horton was not alone in his interest in this unusual locomotive – the gentleman is holding a video camera, and one wonders where the footage is today. *Phil Horton*

Below: **ORTON MERE** We end our section on locomotives with Class 40 No D306 departing from Orton Mere past the Midland Railway signal box. Note the signal wires and point rodding leading from the box and under the line to reach the points, the lattice-post home signal and the circular ground signal on the approach to the station. *Phil Horton*

Mail by rail

Since it opened in 1845 the Nene Valley Railway has always had strong links with the Post Office. In December of that year the Post Office and the London & Birmingham Railway entered into a contract to convey mail over the line, and it did this by transporting not only bags of mail, but an entire horse-drawn coach on a flat wagon. This mail coach had originally run between London and Louth along the Great North Road via Stilton (veering off at Norman Cross), Peterborough, Spalding and

Above: **SUTTON CROSS** The TPO train demonstrates a mailbag pick-up behind Class 47 diesel No 47270. *Brian Sharpe*

Boston. With the arrival of the London & Birmingham Railway at Peterborough, the coach between London and the city was dispensed with, and it ran on the road only between Peterborough and Louth. The journey time for the coach by rail between Euston and Peterborough via Blisworth was less than half of that by road.

At that period of history Wansford Post Office had a status that far outweighed the size of the village. Mail from Wansford was delivered to an area extending over 10 miles, embracing the villages within that radius. As the railways developed and the volume of mail traffic grew, Wansford assumed a new mantle by becoming a Railway Sub Office or RSO. To have this status the greater part of its mail had to be received directly from a Travelling Post Office (TPO). These were the Bletchley to Peterborough and Northampton to Peterborough 'Bag Tenders', with corresponding return workings. Later the vital Peterborough-Rugby-Peterborough mail service was established, carrying huge quantities of mail from Ireland, Wales, the North West and the Midlands into East Anglia and vice versa. These trains also called at Wansford, dropping off and picking up mail, until the end of the First World War.

With the change in postal circulation after this period, Wansford became a rural sub office subordinate to Peterborough, which in turn became one of only 13 General Forwarding Offices in the country. It is this long association between the railways and the Post Office that has been the basis for the Nene Valley Railway's involvement in historic mail by rail activities.

Nene Valley Railway Milestones (7)

1998	Spring	Commercial freight returns to the NVR with 900-tonne pipe trains from Scotland to Yarwell
1998	Summer	New brick-built Ferry Meadows station building completed
2000	August	First mail bag exchange takes place at Sutton Cross
2001	January	Wagons-Lits 'Voiture-Restaurant' No 2975 purchased from Thomas Cook Ltd
2003		Ex-LNER 'B1' Class 4-6-0 No 1306 *Mayflower* returns to steam
2003		Apprentice training scheme launched by GB Railfreight at Wansford
2004		Ex-BR Plasser GB 45-ton TASC track maintenance machine No DR 98500 arrives
2005		BR Standard Class 5 4-6-0 No 73050 *City of Peterborough* returns following overhaul
2007	7 April	Yarwell Junction station opens
2007	1 June	HRH Prince Edward returns for the Railway's 30th Anniversary
2007	June	New heavy overhaul shed opens
2011		HRH Duke of Gloucester becomes Patron of NVR
2012	22 July	Death of the Reverand R. A. Paten
2013	January	Gift shop refurbishment begins
2013	February	Fletton Branch purchase completed
2014	January	*Thomas* withdrawn from service for major overhaul; due to return 2015/6

The first of these was the Railway Letter Service, a scheme that had been established in 1891. An agreement was made between the General Post Office and 79 railway companies, allowing members of the public to post letters at any station for an additional fee. The letter would then be conveyed in the charge of the guard and posted at a distant point. Letters could be 'called for' at a particular station or put into a letter box for delivery in that town. It was an excellent service and, although hard to imagine today, it would be possible to post a letter in the morning and have it delivered the same afternoon! The heritage railway movement continued with this agreement, although it was withdrawn on the national system in 1984. The NVR became party to the agreement in 1986 and has produced its own stamps in increasing numbers ever since. However, the scheme, although fully licensed, is not used in any practical sense, and is now only used to raise funds for the railway. Operated by a dedicated team, the Railway Letter Service continues to flourish and is of great interest to many visitors.

The railway has also been home to a Travelling Post Office (TPO) since around 1977, when the National Railway Museum (NRM) gave permission for

Southern Railway TPO No 4920 to be placed on loan with the NVR, eventually donating it in 2004. In 1995 the NRM decided to dispose of another TPO, and the Nene Valley Railway became home to a second such vehicle in the shape of No M30272M, a Post Office Sorting Carriage. This carriage, the sole surviving vehicle from the 'Great Train Robbery', is now owned by the NVR and requires complete restoration.

This last coach proved to be the catalyst for the formation of a dedicated TPO Group, which is in an advanced stage of restoring No M30272M. The Group has established a fund-raising team, created a comprehensive TPO Archive, issued several publications, and formed a 'Friends' Group to support the aims and activities of the scheme.

In addition, lineside mail bag exchange apparatus equipment has been erected and an education programme developed around the TPO system. An 1885 Great Northern Railway TPO coach body has been donated, and four coaches from the main-line operation, which ceased in 2004, have recently been acquired. The TPO system (1838-2004) will not be allowed to die at the NVR – look out for 'Rail Mail' events, when you can see it for yourself.

Major projects

As can be seen in the 'Nene Valley Railway Milestones' section running through this book, an incredible number of projects have been undertaken and completed over the years, not least during the preservation era.

This section illustrates just a few examples both large and small – including perhaps the biggest of all – that can be found all over the railway, from buildings to postboxes, signals to mileposts and signs, all requiring tender loving

care. Track maintenance, signalling and work in the carriage, wagon and locomotive workshops all play an important and ongoing role in making the visitor experience what it is today and will be in the future. Let's take our hats off to all the staff and volunteers who take up the challenges large and small!

Nene Valley Railway Milestones (8)

2014	April	Refurbishment of Wansford Cafe completed
2014	October	No 73050 *City of Peterborough* withdrawn for major overhaul
2015	February	35A 'New England' Winter Steam Gala marking 50 years since the closure of Peterborough New England locoshed

Father Christmas aboard the Santa Specials

Right and below:
WANSFORD 0-6-0 Pannier Tank No 1501 stands in Wansford station having hauled Santa's train on 14 December 2014. A major winter project, each year the ever popular Santa Special services take a considerable amount of organising but,

as can be seen from Erin Russell's broad smile, brings joy and happiness to excited youngsters!
Frances Townsend

Volunteering

Many visitors are surprised to learn that the Nene Valley Railway, like most private steam railways, is largely a volunteer organisation with only a very small proportion of paid staff. However, you don't have to be a working member to support the railway. Simply by becoming a member you give support and receive a free *Nene Steam* magazine four times per year to keep you informed of all that happens on the NVR. You can attend members' meetings and enjoy concessionary travel.

But have you considered the advantages of active involvement? Working on the railway can be such a refreshing change from day-to-day work. Unwind from the hurly-burly of everyday life by helping to run a friendly private railway. Jobs are available to meet all interests, abilities, ages and tastes, from engine driver to gardener. (Some jobs do, of course, require special training, which you would receive as part of your promotion through the grades.) You could even help with the NVR's 'not so big trains', in the shape of the model railway, which also needs helpers.

Volunteers are not expected to turn up every week; some appear once a month or less, while others come for their summer holidays. The time you give is entirely up to you. Remember that it is possible to stay in a caravan at Ferry Meadows Park, Sacrewell Farm or Yarwell Mill and help the railway at the same time!

As volunteers are the railway's single most valuable asset, they are encouraged to become involved in the running of the railway. The NVR is an educational charity and accredited museum. The railway is heavily dependent on volunteer help. Will you join us? Help is always needed and you are assured of a warm welcome. Please ask for a membership application form (in our timetable) or write to:

The Membership Secretary
Nene Valley Railway
Wansford Station
Stibbington
PETERBOROUGH
PEB 6LR

VOLUNTEERING The NVR relies on the enthusiasm, dedication and hard work of its many volunteers, people like (left to right) a young member, Harry Mallet, Martin Ramm and Ian Watson. *NVR Archive/Peter Townsend*

Right: **WANSFORD** The NVR's little trains at Wansford. *Peter Townsend*

The 'Thomas' story

Although the Nene Valley Railway has bigger and more impressive steam engines, to many visitors and especially children the railway is the home of *Thomas*. Certainly *Thomas* is the NVR's most famous engine and one of its biggest attractions. Few of his friends, however, know how or why *Thomas* received his name.

Hudswell Clarke engine No 1800, an 0-6-0T, was built in 1947 and spent all its working life at the British Sugar Corporation's Peterborough factory. By 1970, when the Peterborough Locomotive Society built its compound within the factory sidings, No 1800 was the regular standby locomotive. Thanks to its immaculate blue livery, it soon became known as *Thomas* to Society members. At the BSC National Sports and Family Day in 1971 and 1972, No 1800 was used to give people short brake-van rides. In

1971 the Reverend W. Awdry, author of the 'Thomas' books, came to one of the Open Days and agreed to name No 1800 *Thomas*.

In 1973 *Thomas* was in need of major repairs and was sold to the Peterborough Railway Society, which stored it out of use until 1977, when parts of a similar locomotive were used to produce one good engine. By 1979 *Thomas* was back in action again. In the past he has visited Didcot, Leicester and Cambridge, promoting the Nene Valley Railway, and has even switched on the Christmas lights in

Peterborough! At Wansford he has attracted more than 8,000 visitors during a single special weekend.

Between 1990 and 1992 *Thomas* received a major overhaul costing in excess of £80,000 and returned to delight children of all ages, frequently working trains on 'Thomas's Branch Line' between Wansford and Yarwell. A further major overhaul was required ten years later, and in 2004 *Thomas* again returned as good as new after £100,000 had been spent making him well. In fact, he felt so 'fit and strong' that the Wansford Controller allowed him to make one return trip to Peterborough each year – a long way for such a small engine!

Above: **WANSFORD** Just some of the many volunteers that help care for *Thomas*.

Right: **YARWELL** Hudswell Clarke 0-6-0T *Thomas* emerges from the Yarwell end of Wansford Tunnel.

Left: **BSC SIDINGS** *Thomas* being named by Rev W. Awdry at the British Sugar Sports & Open Day, June 1971 *All NVR Archive*

During January 2014 *Thomas* retired once again from pulling trains on the NVR to go to 'hospital' for his 10-year overhaul, during which time he will need attention to his boiler, wheels and tanks, and will also receive a new coat of paint. *Thomas*'s overhaul will take more than 12 months to complete and will cost more than £150,000. To help with paying for this very important overhaul the NVR has now launched a Thomas overhaul appeal. While he is in the works one of his friends will be at the NVR to carry on pulling the important trains on *Thomas*'s behalf.

Shops and Cafe

Left and right: **WANSFORD** The NVR's main shop is at Wansford, where a fine selection of books, gifts and souvenirs can be found. The Turntable Cafe was completely refurbished for the start of the 2014 season and offers both indoor and outdoor seating. A selection of meals and light refreshments is served and a visit provides a welcome break between trains. *Peter Townsend*

Above: **FERRY MEADOWS** A small shop is also to be found here within the ticket office. *Peter Townsend*

Below: Class 40 No D306 crosses the Lynch Bridge. *Phil Horton*

Driving Experience Courses

The fire doors are open on USA Class 'S160' No 6046 awaiting the fireman's shovel! *Peter Townsend*

Since 1994, when the world-famous London & North Eastern Railway 'A3' 'Pacific' No 4472 *Flying Scotsman* visited the NVR and the railway offered its first Driving Experience Courses, budding footplate men and women have been given the chance to enjoy the unique sensation of driving a full-sized steam or diesel locomotive. Depending on demand and availability of locomotives, these normally take place on one or two days per month between January and July and between September and November.

Participants are accompanied by one of the NVR's experienced drivers and, after an important safety briefing, receive an insight into how a locomotive works and how it is driven. There is also a visit to the yard and signal box and, of course, an opportunity to use the shovel and operate the controls. Different packages are available and must be booked in advance.

For the beginner there are 2-hour starter courses with just a locomotive (including trips between Wansford and Lynch Bridge, avoiding crossing public roads). For the more experienced there is an advanced course for up to a whole day, working a train of carriages or wagons along the full line, with more than 20 miles of driving.

Driving Experience Courses are ideal gifts for major birthday events, anniversaries and retirement surprises. Although basic fitness is necessary, age is not generally a problem (one gentleman was 90!). Footplate experience can also be part of a corporate hospitality package.

For further details and bookings please contact the NVR office at Wansford station.